remembering 13 July 1985 LIVE AID

The Greatest Show On Earth

Andrew Wild

sonicbondpublishing.com

Sonicbond Publishing Limited
www.sonicbondpublishing.co.uk
Email: info@sonicbondpublishing.co.uk

First Published in the United Kingdom 2024
First Published in the United States 2024

British Library Cataloguing in Publication Data:
A Catalogue record for this book is available from the British Library

ISBN 978-1-78952-328-7

Typeset in ITC Garamond Std & ITC Avant Garde Gothic
Printed and bound in England

Graphic design and typesetting: Full Moon Media

Follow us on social media:
Twitter: https://twitter.com/SonicbondP
Instagram: www.instagram.com/sonicbondpublishing_/
Facebook: www.facebook.com/SonicbondPublishing/

Linktree QR code:

Thank you Nick Jackson

Also by Andrew Wild

Local History

108 Steps Around Macclesfield (Sigma Press, 1994 / 2nd edition, Rumble Strips, 2018)
Exploring Chester (Sigma Press, 1996 / re-publication, Rumble Strips, 2018)
Ever Forward (MADS, 1997)

Biographies

Play On: The Official Biography Of Twelfth Night (Twelfth Night, 2009)
One For The Record: The Official Biography of Galahad (Avalon, 2013 / 2nd edition, 2018)
His Love: Art, Music and Faith. The Official Biography Of Geoff Mann (Sonicbond, 2023)

Books About Music

Pink Floyd Song By Song (Fonthill, 2017)
Queen On Track (Sonicbond, 2018)
The Beatles: An A-Z Guide To Every Song (Sonicbond, 2019)
Solo Beatles 1969-1980 On Track (Sonicbond, 2020)
Crosby, Stills And Nash On Track (Sonicbond, 2020)
Dire Straits On Track (Sonicbond, 2021)
Fleetwood Mac In The 1970s (Sonicbond, 2021)
Eric Clapton Solo On Track (Sonicbond, 2021)
Eric Clapton Sessions (Sonicbond, 2022)
Phil Collins In The 1980s (Sonicbond, 2022)
The Allman Brothers Band On Track (Sonicbond, 2022)
Four Sides Of The Circle (Rumble Strips, 2024)
A Mirror Of Dreams: The Progressive Rock Revival 1981 To 1983 (Kingmaker, 2024)
A Playground Of Broken Hearts: The Progressive Rock Revival 1984 To 1989 (Kingmaker, 2025)

Books About Films

James Bond On Screen (Sonicbond, 2022)

Books About Comics

The Perfect Marvel Comics Collection – 1939-1985 (Rumble Strips, 2022)

Plays

The Difficult Crossing (Stagescripts, 2016)
A Difficult Man (Rumble Strips, 2021)

Author's Note

Unless otherwise stated, all quotes attributed to Bob Geldof are taken from his autobiography *Is That It?* (1986).

All author royalties for this book will be donated to the Band Aid Charitable Trust, charity number 292199.

> Bob Geldof was on our case like a Rottweiler in a cattery. His tenacity and passion for the cause were demonic and angelic all at once.
> John Illsley, *My Life In Dire Straits* (2021)

> I set up an area backstage with fake grass and a barbecue so other artists could drop by. Freddie Mercury arrived, still on a high from Queen's show-stealing performance and offered a very Freddie-esque appraisal of the hat I'd chosen to perform in: 'Darling! What the fuck were you wearing on your head? You looked like the Queen Mother!'
> Elton John, *Me* (2019)

> Live Aid is perhaps the most famous concert ever staged and celebrated the superstars created in the rock era. The exact sum of money raised for Ethiopian famine relief from the individual donations phoned in during the shows is impossible to document with academic accuracy but seems to have been well over £100 million, to which can be added the income from concert ticket sales, programme and advertising sales, broadcasting and DVD rights, and so forth.
> Simon Frith, Matt Brennan, Martin Cloonan and Emma Webster,
> *The History of Live Music In Britain, Volume 3, 1985-2015* (2021)

remembering LIVE AID

Contents

Would you like to write for Sonicbond Publishing?

At Sonicbond Publishing we are always on the look-out for authors, particularly for our two main series:

On Track. Mixing fact with in depth analysis, the On Track series examines the work of a particular musical artist or group. All genres are considered from easy listening and jazz to 60s soul to 90s pop, via rock and metal.

On Screen. This series looks at the world of film and television. Subjects considered include directors, actors and writers, as well as entire television and film series. As with the On Track series, we balance fact with analysis.

While professional writing experience would, of course, be an advantage the most important qualification is to have real enthusiasm and knowledge of your subject. First-time authors are welcomed, but the ability to write well in English is essential.

Sonicbond Publishing has distribution throughout Europe and North America, and all books are also published in E-book form. Authors will be paid a royalty based on sales of their book.

Further details are available from www.sonicbondpublishing.co.uk. To contact us, complete the contact form there or email info@sonicbondpublishing.co.uk

Introduction

On Saturday 13 July 1985, three weeks past my 19th birthday, I settled in front of the television in our small semi-detached house in Stockport. It was just before noon in London, 7 am in Philadelphia, and around the world, it was time for Live Aid. Sixteen hours later, I was still there, having watched the entire BBC broadcast from end to end (with a small gap during George Thorogood's set in the early evening to fetch my tea). I also taped around three hours of the BBC Radio 1 broadcast onto two C90 cassettes: as I recall, I snagged sets from Dire Straits, The Who, Santana, Freddie Mercury And Brian May, Paul McCartney, Band Aid, Neil Young, Eric Clapton, Led Zeppelin, Patti LaBelle, Mick Jagger and Bob Dylan. Not so far away, my future wife and her sisters were doing much the same – watching, taping and making indelible memories.

Years later, I found a 17xCD bootleg set of every available audio recording from the London and Philadelphia shows – there was significant overlap in performances on the day, and the first three hours from Philadelphia were not broadcast in the UK at all, so even though I'd sat through the entire broadcast, what I'd seen was far from complete. This bootleg filled in many of the gaps. Much of the video footage from both concerts is available on YouTube.

This book revisits the seventy-plus artists and close to 200 songs that made up Live Aid. How much of it do you remember? For my generation, 13 July 1985 was a landmark day. It was 'The Greatest Show On Earth'.

Andrew Wild
Rainow, Cheshire, 2024

Prologue: Do They Know It's Christmas?

It's Tuesday, 23 October 1984. Images of hundreds of thousands of people starving to death in Ethiopia are shown on the UK's BBC TV news bulletins. Michael Buerk described it as 'a biblical famine in the 20th century' and 'the closest thing to hell on Earth'. Buerk in the *Guardian,* 2004:

> I was based in Johannesburg at the time and was the BBC's correspondent in Africa. The rains that should have come in around August to Ethiopia had failed again for the sixth season running and it tipped over from being a crisis to a catastrophe. People suddenly realised they were going to die and this huge mass migration started. It tipped very quickly. We flew and then drove up there and the roads were just littered with dying people. It was extraordinary; it was just on such a huge scale.

Buerk noted that at Korem, there were 40,000-45,000 people, and in Makele, there were another 80,000-90,000. He remembered that they grouped along the road that led north from Addis, where they thought relief would get to them.

> It's difficult to express the inadequacy I felt. You take refuge in the technicalities of filming, finding sequences, working out the logistics and so on. There were two films, two pieces that finally aired. I knew they wanted about three minutes, but I cut eight and thought, fuck 'em. In those days as a foreign correspondent, communications being what they were, I tended to work on the basis that they got what they were given. I knew it was a very powerful film.

Irish musician Bob Geldof, the outspoken and fiercely intelligent singer with The Boomtown Rats, saw the broadcast at home in London. He had spent the day promoting the band's upcoming single 'Dave', the third single from their latest album *In The Long Grass,* which was six months old and a decided flop. He recalled later that he was resigned to the decline of a band he'd led for nine years. He went home and switched on the television. The news report was of famine in Ethiopia. He wrote, later:

> I saw something that placed my worries in a ghastly new perspective. From the first seconds, it was clear that this was a horror on a monumental scale. The pictures were of people who were so shrunken by starvation that they looked like beings from another planet. Their arms and legs were as thin as sticks, their bodies spindly. Swollen veins and huge, blankly staring eyes protruded from their shrivelled heads. The camera wandered amidst them like a mesmerised observer, occasionally dwelling on one person so that he looked directly at me, sitting in my comfortable living room surrounded by the fripperies of modern living, which we were pleased to regard as necessities. Their eyes looked into mine.

Unable to sleep, Geldof mused on how he might be able to help.

> To allow it to continue would be tantamount to murder. I would send some money; I would send more money. But that was not enough. What else could I do? I was only a pop singer. And, by now, not a very successful pop singer. I could not help the tottering man to carry his burden. All I could do was make records that no one bought. But I would do that, I would give all the profits of the next Rats record to Oxfam. What good would that do? It would be a pitiful amount. But it would be more than I could raise by simply dipping into my shrunken bank account. Maybe some people would buy it just because the profits were for Oxfam. Yet, that was still not enough. I fell into a fitful sleep.

The next day, Geldof's partner, the broadcaster Paula Yates, had been in Newcastle filming an episode of *The Tube* with Ultravox's Midge Ure. 'After the show, I dropped into Paula's dressing room for a natter.'

Yates was chatting on the phone with Geldof. She handed Ure the phone and Geldof asked him if he'd seen the TV reporty about the famine in Ethiopia. Ure confessed that he hadn't. Gelodof explained about how he wanted to do something about it and asked Ure to help. Ure agreed and they agreed to meet up a few days later at Langan's Brasserie in Mayfair.

Ure wrote:

> Over the weekend, I made a point of watching the reports from Ethiopia. They were all over the box, so I couldn't miss it. I found it horrific that we should be seeing images like that in this day and age, but I also couldn't escape the feeling that anything I did would be nothing more than an empty gesture. At Langan's, Bob and I talked around a bunch of bizarre schemes before coming to the obvious conclusion that the only thing we could do was make a record. The quickest option – covering somebody else's song like 'White Christmas' – was out of the question because almost half of the monies earned by a record go to the writer. There we were, two songwriters sitting at the same table arguing over which old chestnut we could cover when, eventually, we realised that what we had to do was to write and record a new song and that we only had a few weeks left before Christmas. Initially, we calculated that if we came up with something, invited our friends to sing on it and managed to get a hit, we could raise £100,000. I told him, 'You are a songwriter; just write a song.' I was his backstop, his credibility; once I'd agreed to write with him, he could tell people, 'Midge and I are writing the song together.'

Ure went home and started work on what would become the 'feed the world' chorus of 'Do They Know It's Christmas?'. Geldof, for his part, phoned Sting and Simon Le Bon, who said yes, then headed towards the Picasso bar in

Chelsea to look for well-known musicians. On the way, he bumped into Gary Kemp of Spandau Ballet. Kemp said:

> I was in an antique store [Antiquarius] on the King's Road. Geldof saw me and came in. He sucked the air out of the place and took over, as he does. He said, 'Did you see the news?' He was clearly very moved. 'Maybe if we got a few people together, yourselves, Duran and some others, would you be interested in making a record?' I said yeah, sure and that was it.

Reassured, Geldof opened his address book and started to make calls. 'I called Virgin records to get the number for Boy George', he wrote. 'I rang ZTT for Frankie Goes To Hollywood. I got hold of numbers for Paul Young, Paul Weller of The Style Council and Phil Oakey of The Human League.' He bumped into Francis Rossi of Status Quo in the offices of their mutual record company. And, needing the kernel of a song, he reworked an unfinished Boomtown Rats track called 'It's My World', and thus, the verses of 'Do They Know It's Christmas?' were in place. Geldof and Ure later worked together on the middle eight and the 'let them know it's Christmas time' refrain. There is no chorus. One can argue that the lyrics are patronising, and to a degree, they are, but they're simple, catchy and memorable.

Geldof and Ure wanted Trevor Horn to produce the recording sessions, but Horn was unable to commit to such a tight schedule. Instead, Horn donated his Sarm West Studios in Notting Hill, London, for recording sessions. Geldof and Ure were given 24 hours to record and mix the single. The date: Sunday 25 November 1984. 'Trevor would have taken six weeks to produce it', Ure said, who elected to produce the single himself. 'I enjoy the pressure of a deadline and I'm good at dealing with artists.'

The basic track was recorded by Ure in his home studio in Chiswick, with some vocals laid down on the day before the Sarm sessions. John Taylor of Duran Duran provided bass guitar and Paul Weller played a guitar part that was ultimately mixed out.

'On the Sunday morning, Bob and I pitched up first', Ure wrote:

> The studio was just off Portobello Road. At eight o'clock in the morning, the whole area is usually empty, filthy and damp, suffering from a Saturday night hangover. On this Sunday, the world's media were standing outside, TV crews and photographers poking cameras in my face, journalists waving microphones. There was no one else inside the studio. Not a single star in sight. Bob looked at me. 'If it's only The Boomtown Rats and Ultravox,' he said, 'it's going to be a fucking dull record.'

Geldof had no certainty that anyone would come. But people started to arrive.

'Most people looked as if they had just got out of bed,' he wrote, 'which, by and large, they had. I remember seeing Sting strolling up the street half-reading his Sunday paper, Paul Weller, all nervous energy, emerging striding from the opposite direction and Marilyn flouncing around the corner like a beautiful starlet on her way to the corner shop to buy some milk. I looked around and saw that the room held most of the stars of British pop music. They looked like a bunch of yobs down the pub on a Sunday lunchtime.'

'Drinking pints of milk in a valiant attempt to cure our persistent hangovers,' writes Heaven 17's Martyn Ware, 'we stumbled towards the studio only to be confronted by an unimaginable scene. There were multiple TV crews and their remote vans, journalists, artists arriving by the truckload with their entourages, security guards – the lot. Glenn [Gregory] and I had no idea where to go, but we were hustled into the studio away from the crazy hubbub outside.' 'Midge phoned me the night before', Gregory said. 'Martyn and I lived literally around the corner, so we could walk there the next day. I hope that's not the only reason we were asked.'

Spandau Ballet and Duran Duran flew into London from Germany, where they had appeared on a TV show together. Ure: 'The studio reception was packed with the biggest artists that the UK had to offer in 1984: Paul Young, Spandau Ballet, Wham!, Duran Duran and Bananarama. 'Bananarama shared record company offices with The Boomtown Rats', Keren Woodward told *Classic Pop Presents* in 2023. 'Bob came up to us and said, 'I'm doing a charity thing, will you do it?' We had no idea of the scale of it, but I don't think anyone did. If I had known, I might not have turned up to the recording with a hangover, wearing an old grey jumper with my hair in a ponytail.'

'There were a few strange ones', Ure recalled. 'Hot American funk band Kool And The Gang, who happened to be in town, and Francis Rossi and Rick Parfitt from Status Quo.' Rossi:

> I have to confess that Rick and I were nervous about turning up at Sarm West that day. We had only met Geldof once before, bumping into him at the offices of Phonogram. We didn't know most of the others. We wondered if they would just see us as these incredibly old farts like Mum and Dad turning up and ruining the kids' party. We needn't have worried, though. Everyone was as nice as pie. It turned out that the first gig Paul Weller ever went to was to see Quo perform. He said it was so loud and exciting; it was the final clincher in his decision to form his own band.

Mark Ellen, editor of *Smash Hits,* was one of just two journalists present. 'A shrieking Bananarama queued at the coffee machine with Francis Rossi', he wrote later:

> A quiet, fizzing tension filled the air, everyone trying to work out the pecking order or finding some distraction that made them look cool and detached. Nick Rhodes stuck some money in the Asteroids machine. John Taylor ordered chilli con carne. Weller and Bananarama watched a TV

set with the sound off. Status Quo, the Duran rhythm section and some Boomtown Rats found cans of lager and went out for a smoke. The briefly chart-troubling Marilyn appeared uninvited, but he came anyway.

The group choruses were recorded first, as Ure and Geldof decided who would take which parts of each line. 'One by one,' Ellen observed, 'the lead singers were summoned for their parts. Tony Hadley stepped up first and I felt for him. Could any audience be more terrifying than his peers and chart rivals squinting from the control room? The whole thing had the undercurrent of a penalty shoot-out: they had to put one away for the team but also, ideally, ram as much of their own personality into their few seconds as possible.'

Boy George arrived from New York after an appearance on *Late Night With David Letterman*. 'The Band Aid event was one of the few times I've felt comfortable around other pop stars', he wrote in *Take It Like A Man*. 'It was as if everybody had deflated their egos for the evening. It all seemed very natural. There was no banquet laid on for the stars, just cups of tea and coffee and bacon and cheese sandwiches.'

Perhaps inevitably, Phil Collins plays drums. 'I turned up expecting the band to be George Michael, Sting, Bob Geldof, Midge Ure and me on drums', Collins wrote in *Not Dead Yet*. 'Instead, there was this assembled Who's Who. I'd met Sting before, and always thought he was hip and I wasn't, but we struck up a friendship that day.'

Sting: 'It was a funny day, like a school reunion for truants. All of us had a lot in common but had rarely been in the same room together. There were no fights, as I remember.'

Ure: 'The hardest part was not getting people there but getting them to leave.'

Francis Rossi: 'What I hadn't expected was how much many of us had in common when it came to cocaine. Naturally, Rick and I had ensured we would get through the day feeling as little pain as possible and brought our own not-inconsiderable supplies. Very soon, our little corner of the studio became the go-to hangout for quite a few others.'

Martyn Ware: 'The legend of that session is that the 'bad boys' – i.e. Spandau Ballet, Status Quo and us – were on the hunt for pharmaceutical enhancement, but I can confirm that this wasn't the case.'

Rossi: 'As the day flashed by and Rick and I were finally called to add our vocals, poor old Rick had shoved so much powder up his hooter, his voice had cracked. So, I ended up overdubbing his part. It didn't make any difference. I'd had Rick's voice singing in my ears for nearly 20 years, so I could do a passable imitation. Being Rick the rock star, he did manage to push himself right to the front for the group picture afterwards though, standing next to Sting like they were the best mates in all the world.'

Recording finished mid-evening. The featured vocalists, in order of appearance, are:

Paul Young: It's Christmas time, there's no need to be afraid. At Christmas time, we let in light and we banish shade
Boy George: And in our world of plenty, we can spread a smile of joy. Throw your arms around the world at Christmastime
George Michael: But say a prayer. Pray for the other ones. At Christmas time…
Simon Le Bon: …it's hard, but when you're having fun, there's a world outside your window
Simon Le Bon with Sting: And it's a world of dread and fear
Sting with Tony Hadley: Where the only water flowing is the bitter sting of tears
Sting with Bono: And the Christmas bells that ring there are the clanging chimes of doom
Bono: Well tonight thank God it's them instead of you
Boy George, Sting, Bono and Paul Young, with Midge Ure, Paul Weller and Glenn Gregory: And there won't be snow in Africa this Christmas time. The greatest gift they'll get this year is life. Where nothing ever grows, no rain or rivers flow, do they know it's Christmas time at all?
Glenn Gregory with Marilyn: Here's to you
Paul Young: Raise a glass for everyone
Glenn Gregory and Marilyn: Here's to them
Paul Young: Underneath that burning sun
Paul Young, Marilyn & Glenn Gregory: Do they know it's Christmas time at all?

Other artists who contribute to massed group vocals include Jody Whatley of Shalamar and members of Bananarama, The Boomtown Rats, Culture Club, Duran Duran, Heaven 17, Spandau Ballet, Status Quo, U2 and Ultravox.

The song was mixed throughout the night. The B-side, an instrumental version, features spoken messages from some of the artists who couldn't take part, including Big Country, Holly Johnson of Frankie Goes To Hollywood, David Bowie and Paul McCartney.

The master went immediately to the pressing plant, and Geldof took a cassette to BBC Radio 1, where it was played on Simon Bates' mid-morning show. The single was released on 3 December under the group name Band Aid. Geldof persuaded Michael Grade, then controller of BBC 1, to broadcast a special screening ahead of that week's *Top Of The Pops*. Bob Geldof asked David Bowie to introduce it as he had been unable to take part in the recording of the song. 'Bowie arrived fashionably late with his PA', Midge Ure recalled. 'We all stood up as if the headmaster had arrived. Everyone turned into giggling fans, hanging on his every word. He readily agreed to introduce the single, even though he'd have to cut off the goatee he'd started growing to enable him to go out shopping in London without being recognised.'

'Do They Know It's Christmas?' was an immediate number one, staying on top of the charts for five weeks. The songs raised £8 million, staying in the charts for the whole of 1985 and spawning re-recordings in 1989, 2004 and 2014. It remains the second best-selling single *ever* in the UK. 'I'd expected

Band Aid would be for that one Christmas and never heard of again', Geldof told *Classic Pop*. 'We'd give Oxfam a couple of hundred grand and that's it, the most we could do. Millions of sales later, it was a phenomenon. I got a bit scared, but I said I'd ride it out and I did.'

Band Aid has raised over £100 million. Geldof, unsurprisingly, has no truck with anyone who questions the lyrics:

> What about it isn't politically correct? There won't be snow in Africa this Christmastime? Well, there won't be. Extinction Rebellion will tell you that. I couldn't give a fuck, it's nonsense. Criticise it from a musical point of view, say it's a shit pop song, whatever, okay. But still today, Europe is the richest continent in the world, when it's eight miles from the poorest. Still today, Africa is open to being pillaged. I work every day on Band Aid, so anyone who says it's not politically correct: go fuck yourself.

Elsewhere, 'Do They Know It's Christmas?' topped the charts in Australia, Austria, Belgium, Canada, Denmark, Ireland, Italy, The Netherlands, New Zealand, Norway, Sweden, Switzerland and West Germany, as well as landing just outside the top ten in the US.

"Do They Know It's Christmas?' stands apart from the rest of my career', says Midge Ure. 'It was both a purely selfless act and the most cold, calculated thing I've ever done in my life. It is a song that has nothing to do with music. It was all about generating money – get the artists there, make this event happen, get the cameras there, it will sell. That was the mantra. The names were much more important than the song. The song didn't matter: the song was secondary, almost irrelevant.'

The song was number one in the UK over Christmas and Bob Geldof arranged a group performance for *Top Of The Pops*. Paul Young, Boy George, Simon Le Bon, Sting, Tony Hadley and Paul Weller (miming Bono's part) take the spotlight. Dozens of other pop stars join in the chorus, including some of those who took part in the original recording – Status Quo, Midge Ure and Phil Collins – and many who didn't.

Just before Christmas, on 22 December 1984, Culture Club played the last date of a UK tour at Wembley Arena. As a finale, George Michael, Tony Hadley, Marilyn, Paul Young and Elton John joined Culture Club on stage for 'Do They Know It's Christmas?'. Bob Geldof was also present and Boy George suggested to him that they should consider organising a benefit concert. Speaking to *Melody Maker* at the beginning of January 1985, Geldof said:

> It's a logical progression from the record. The show should be as big as is humanly possible. There's no point in just 5,000 fans turning up at Wembley; we need to have Wembley linked with Madison Square Gardens and the whole show to be televised worldwide. It would be great for Duran Duran to play three or four numbers at Wembley and then flick to Madison

> Square, where Springsteen would be playing. While he's on, the Wembley stage could be made ready for the next British act. In that way, lots of acts could be featured and the television rights, tickets and so on could raise a phenomenal amount of money. It's not an impossible idea, and certainly one worth exploiting.

Here, six months before the concerts, Geldof has laid down the Live Aid manifesto.

Meanwhile, many other countries recorded their own charity singles. France gave us 'Éthiopie' by Chanteurs Sans Frontières, written by Renaud Séchan, one of France's most popular singers, and producer Franck Langolff. This topped the French singles chart for two months and is relentlessly horrible. Ireland's 'Show Some Concern' by The Concerned is laughably bad. The upbeat 'Starvation' by the mixed-race collective Starvation comprises UB40, Madness, The Pioneers, The Specials, General Public, Dick Cuthell, Annie Whitehead and Afrodiziak. Wisely, they choose a cover version, thus avoiding the self-conscious lyrics evident elsewhere. Better still, the B-side, 'Tam Tam Pour L'Ethiopie' – nine minutes on its 12" version – gathers artists from across Africa. Vocalists include King Sunny Adé, Zao, André Marie Tala, M'pongo Lave, Pamelo, Malopoets, Hugh Masekela and Youssou N'Dour. The lyrics were sung in a mixture of African languages, including Douala, Lingala, Wolof, Malinke and Swahili. Proceeds from the record were distributed to the charities Oxfam, War On Want and Médecins Sans Frontières. A supergroup of Latin American and Spanish singers, Proyecto Hermanos, produced 'Cantaré, Cantarás', which sounds like 'We Are The World' in Spanish but with Ricardo Montalban and Julio Iglesias replacing Bob Dylan and Ray Charles. In Quebec, Fondation Québec-Afrique's 'Les Yeux De La Faim' gathered a large number of French-Canadian artists. Heavy metal stars donated 'Stars' by Hear 'N Aid. This features vocals and mid-80s perms from Ronnie James Dio (who co-wrote the song) and members of Y&T, Judas Priest, Quiet Riot, Blue Öyster Cult, Rough Cutt, Queensrÿche and Dokken. It includes an ear-bending 20 guitar solos and went to number one in Norway. In direct contrast, 'One Big Family' by Heart Of Nashville includes vocal turns from country stars George Jones, Eddy Arnold, Faron Young, Tanya Tucker, Dobie Gray, Ray Sawyer (the eye-patched guy from Dr. Hook), Lynn Anderson, Bobby Bare, The Kendalls, The Jordanaires, Ronnie McDowell and 82-year-old Roy Acuff. There is no guitar solo but much emoting and, yes, an obligatory trucker-driver modulation. Possibly worst of the lot is 'Volare' by Musicitalia, in which 22 Italian artists of questionable talent and dubious fashion sense bury the song usually known as 'Nel Blu, Dipinto Di Blu' under many kilogrammes of *formaggio*. Less awful is 'Tears Are Not Enough', which was written by celebrated Canadian producer David Foster, with lyrics by Bryan Adams and his musical partner Jim Vallance. The track was recorded in Toronto on 10 February 1985. The solo vocalists, in order, are Gordon Lightfoot, Burton

Cummings (Guess Who), Anne Murray, Joni Mitchell, Dan Hill, Neil Young, Bryan Adams, Corey Hart, Bruce Cockburn, Geddy Lee (Rush) and Mike Reno (Loverboy). Many other Canadian names provide duo, trio or chorus vocals. Fist-pumping is in evidence. Released in May 1985 under the group name Northern Lights, it was the best-selling Canadian single of the year.

However, perhaps the most celebrated was USA For Africa's 'We Are The World'. The project was initiated by Harry Belafonte, who enlisted manager Ken Kragen, who asked his clients Lionel Richie and Kenny Rogers to participate. Quincy Jones was drafted in to co-produce the song. Jones brought in Michael Jackson. Jackson and Richie wrote 'We Are The World' together across a week of composing sessions. With a backing track prepared a few days beforehand, the vocals were recorded on 28 January 1985 at A&M Studios, Hollywood. Many of the participants came straight from an American Music Awards ceremony hosted by Lionel Richie at the Shrine Auditorium in Los Angeles.

The soloists, in order of appearance, are:

Lionel Richie: There comes a time when we heed a certain call
Lionel Richie and Stevie Wonder: When the world must come together as one
Stevie Wonder: There are people dying
Paul Simon: Oh, and it's time to lend a hand to life
Paul Simon and Kenny Rogers: The greatest gift of all
Kenny Rogers: We can't go on pretending day by day
James Ingram: That someone, somewhere will soon make a change
Tina Turner: We are all a part of God's great big family
Billy Joel: And the truth, you know,
Tina Turner and Billy Joel: love is all we need
Michael Jackson: We are the world, we are the children. We are the ones who make a brighter day so let's start giving
Diana Ross: There's a choice we're making, we're saving our own lives
Michael Jackson and Diana Ross: It's true, we'll make a better day, just you and me
Dionne Warwick: Well, send them your heart so they'll know that someone cares
Dionne Warwick and Willie Nelson: And their lives will be stronger and free
Willie Nelson: As God has shown us by turning stone to bread
Al Jarreau: And so, we all must lend a helping hand
Bruce Springsteen: We are the world, we are the children
Kenny Loggins: We are the ones who make a brighter day, so let's start giving
Steve Perry: Oh, there's a choice we're making, we're saving our own lives
Daryl Hall: It's true, we'll make a better day, just you and me
Michael Jackson: When you're down and out, and there seems no hope at all
Huey Lewis: But if you just believe, there's no way we can fall
Cyndi Lauper: Well, well, well, let us realise, oh, that a change can only come
Kim Carnes When we…
Huey Lewis and Kim Carnes: …stand together as one

Choir: We are the world, we are the children, we are the ones who make a brighter day so let's start giving. There's a choice we're making, we're saving our own lives. It's true, we'll make a better day just you and me. We are the world, we are the children, we are the ones who make a brighter day so let's start giving.

Bob Dylan: There's a choice we're making, we're saving our own lives. It's true, we'll make a better day, just you and me

Choir: We are the world. We are the children. We are the ones who make a brighter day, so let's start giving. There's a choice we're making, we're saving our own lives

Bob Dylan: It's true, we'll make a better day, just you and me

Ray Charles: Alright, let me hear you

Choir: We are the world

Ray Charles: We are the world

Choir: We are the children

Ray Charles: Yeah, we are the children

Choir: We are the ones who make a brighter day, so let's start giving

Ray Charles: Let's start giving. There's a choice we're making. We're saving our own lives, It's true, we'll make a better day just you and me. Come on, y'all, let me hear you

Stevie Wonder: We are the world

Bruce Springsteen: We are the world

Stevie Wonder: We are the children

Bruce Springsteen: We are the children

Stevie Wonder: We are the ones who make a brighter day, so let's start giving

Bruce Springsteen: So let's start giving

Stevie Wonder: There's a choice we're making, we're saving our own lives. It's true, we'll make a better day, just you and me, yeah, yeah. We are the world

Bruce Springsteen: We are the world

Stevie Wonder: We are the children

Bruce Springsteen: We are the children

Stevie Wonder: We are the ones who make a brighter day, so let's start giving

Bruce Springsteen: So let's start giving. There's a choice we're making. We're saving our own lives. It's true, we'll make a better day. Just you and me

Choir: We are the world, we are the children. We are the ones who make a brighter day. So let's start giving. There's a choice we're making, we're saving our own lives. It's true, we'll make a better day, just you and me

James Ingram: We are the world, we are the children. We are the ones who make a brighter day so let's start giving

Ray Charles: There's a choice we're making. We're saving our own lives. It's true, we'll make a better day, just you and me

Choir: We are the world, we are the children, we are the ones who make a brighter day, so let's start giving. There's a choice we're making. We're saving our own lives. It's true, we'll make a better day, just you and me

Each, in turn, attempts to out-sing the others, except for Dylan, who looks as though he'd prefer to be somewhere else. The massed chorus added Dan Aykroyd, Harry Belafonte, Lindsey Buckingham, Sheila E., The Jacksons, Waylon Jennings, Bette Midler, John Oates, Jeffrey Osborne, The Pointer Sisters, Smokey Robinson and members of Huey Lewis And The News. Bob Geldof attended the sessions. Too overawed to sing, he spent the evening taking photographs and chatting to Bob Dylan.

Released on 7 March, 'We Are The World' was a four-week number one in the US in April and May. For two of these, it was at the top of the UK charts and was number one in Australia, France, Ireland, New Zealand, The Netherlands, Norway, Sweden and Switzerland.

The next logical step? A benefit concert. 'I am not certain when the Live Aid idea was first planted,' Geldof wrote, 'and I could not know that it would turn out to be the biggest fund-raising event, the biggest TV event and the biggest concert in history. Had I known this from the outset, I might never have had the nerve to begin.' As The Boomtown Rats fulfilled touring commitments in the early months of 1985, Geldof got to work. He hooked up with promoter Harvey Goldsmith. 'I didn't really get a chance to say no', Goldsmith told the *Guardian* in 2004. 'Bob arrived in my office and basically said, "We're doing this." It started from there.'

The first to agree to take part was Nik Kershaw, who bumped into Geldof at Heathrow. From this inauspicious beginning, Geldof set his sights on bigger names. The stories of how he bluffed artists to agree to play are legion. 'People now say, how could an artist refuse to be on a show like that?' production manager Andy Zweck told the *Guardian*. 'But my memory prior to the event was how Bob and Harvey Goldsmith struggled to get the artists and struggled to get the show in America. Bob had to play some tricks to get artists involved. He had to call Elton and say, "Queen are in and Bowie's in", and, of course, they weren't. Then, he'd call Bowie and say Elton and Queen are in. It was a game of bluff.'

'Bob has this amazing talent to cut through the social formalities', says Midge Ure. 'It was like watching this Tasmanian Devil hack its way through a jungle: he just went through trees and whatever was in his way.'

Bob Geldof: 'When I announced it, the only one who was dithering, as ever, was Bryan Ferry. So I just said, " ... and Bryan Ferry." And he rang to say, "I didn't say yeah." I said, "Well, say no, then. You're the one who can announce it, though."'

'Geldof's powers of persuasion [were] extraordinary', writes Mark Ellen:

> If an act had dragged their heels about taking part, he'd remind them that less money would be raised as a consequence and more people would die, many of them children. He stopped short of saying their non-appearance would condemn those helpless Africans to an early grave; he left that hanging in the air, but the vast majority signed up and the few who declined may have spent a chunk of their lives feeling bad about it.

By mid-April, legendary American promotor Bill Graham was starting to plan out the US concert. After a number of venues were deemed unsuitable, Graham settled on the John F Kennedy Stadium in Philadelphia. Built in 1926 as the Philadelphia Municipal Stadium, it was renamed in 1964. Since then, the venue has hosted some major concerts, including The Beatles (16 August 1966), Judy Garland (20 July 1968), a Bicentennial Concert featuring Yes and Peter Frampton (12 June 1976), The Rolling Stones (25 and 26 September 1981), Foreigner and The Kinks (19 June 1982), Blondie (21 August 1982), The Who (25 September 1982), The Police (20 August 1983) and The Jacksons (1, 2, 28 and 30 September 1984).

Bill Graham: 'I had used JFK for The Stones in 1981 and the backstage area was huge… the stadium held a hundred thousand people. I went back there to look at it again and it was good.'

With both venues finally confirmed, the Live Aid concerts were announced on 10 June 1985, with tickets selling at £5 (with a £20 donation to reduce the tax burden) or $35 each. The promotional posters show all of the anticipated acts in alphabetical order and many more were added to both halves of the show before and on the day. Despite being advertised, Boy George, Tears For Fears, Billy Joel, Huey Lewis And The News, Waylon Jennings and Stevie Wonder did not take part.

Midge Ure: 'We couldn't get any black superstar to perform at either concert and it wasn't for lack of trying. We asked Prince, Stevie Wonder, Diana Ross and Michael Jackson, who were all otherwise engaged or not interested in doing it. As a result, a wealth of American artists missed out on being part of Live Aid.'

Bill Graham: 'I contacted every single major black artist … they all turned down Live Aid. [Local promoter] Larry Magid was a great help. He knew a lot of the black acts and we got The Four Tops, Teddy Pendergrass, Ashford And Simpson and Patti LaBelle.'

'*Black Voice,* the black community newspaper mainly known for the excitable nature of its reporting and journalists, was calling Live Aid the racist event of the decade', Geldof wrote in his memoirs:

> The thing that bothered me was that these same people had never done a story on the famine, nor were they interested in doing anything to help those people. They were only interested in the very thing they accused others of. I was still as opposed to tokenism as I had been during the punk period. I wasn't interested in Uncle Tommery, having a black man there because he was black. Who cares? I wasn't interested in having an African on simply because he was African – he could have been Outer Mongolian for all I cared if he sold a million records. I was interested in pragmatics. I was interested in making money to prevent people from dying. 'Would you help if the black bands put on their own concert?' they asked. 'Absolutely.' I heard no more.

Bill Graham recounts how, as the list of confirmed acts grew, other bands wanted to be involved. Kris Kristofferson, Yes and Foreigner were told, 'no'. Paul Simon pulled out. Ozzy Osbourne wanted to rejoin Black Sabbath. Graham extended the show forward to start at 9 am. 'I made a slot for Black Sabbath at 11 in the morning', he wrote. 'Can you imagine looking at Ozzy Osbourne at 11 in the morning? Following The Four Tops?'

Bruce Springsteen had just finished a five-week leg of his *Born In The USA* tour with three nights at Wembley Stadium (3, 4 and 6 July) and Roundhay Park in Leeds (7 July) ahead of some downtime with his new wife, Julianne, six weeks after their wedding. Geldof courted him, both on the phone and in person. 'We talked about everything except what it was necessary to talk about', Geldof said. 'I was told later by a mutual friend that Springsteen regretted not sticking the guitar in the back seat and coming down. Pity.' Springsteen agreed to leave his stage in situ at Wembley for the Live Aid concert but surely regrets not driving the 70 miles to Philadelphia, especially as three British acts, The Pretenders, Simple Minds and Duran Duran, flew to the US at their own expense to ensure they could take part.

There were other notable absentees. Frankie Goes To Hollywood spent 36 weeks in the UK top ten in 1984, 15 of them at number one. In February 1985, 'Relax' was awarded Best British Single of 1984 and won the Brit Award for British Breakthrough Act. But they had just left the UK to spend a year in Ireland to reduce their tax burden. Culture Club enjoyed seven consecutive top-five UK hits and six in the US between 1982 and 1984. Singer Boy George was developing a debilitating drug habit, which would eventually split the band. Eurythmics, Rod Stewart, Talking Heads, AC/DC, Def Leppard, Paul Simon, Liza Minnelli, Yoko Ono and Cyndi Lauper were all invited but chose not to be involved. Frank Zappa refused to take part, later telling Howard Stern that Live Aid was 'the biggest cocaine money-laundering scheme of all time.'

Big Country, Marillion and The Moody Blues were keen but too late; however, Stuart Adamson, Bruce Watson, Mark Brzezicki, Fish, Justin Hayward and John Lodge rocked up at Wembley anyway, as did Hazel O'Connor and Nils Lofgren. Cat Stevens arrived at Wembley uninvited. Speaking to the *Radio Times* in August 2020, he said: 'I turned up without my guitar and I think they were a bit worried about what I might do. I was going to read a poem. It was a good poem, but I think they were probably right not to have me. I was left out of it. I didn't mind. They made the right decision.'

The Sun, that trusted arbiter of truth and wisdom, ran the following entirely fictional article on 12 July, the day before the concert:

> Beatles in Live Aid reunion: Fab 3 plus Julian
> The Beatles are poised to play together in a dramatic reunion tomorrow, with Julian Lennon replacing his murdered father. The secret bid to reunite the world's greatest-ever pop group for the finale of the Live Aid concert

got underway yesterday. It started after George Harrison flew into London's Heathrow Airport. The Wembley finale – scheduled for just before 10 pm – will include 43-year-old McCartney singing the last Beatle hit, 'Let It Be'. It will be a moment of rock history if Julian, 22, George Harrison, 42, and Ringo Starr, 45, join him to re-create the famous sound.

It seems likely that McCartney, Harrison and Starr did indeed discuss a Live Aid appearance. As soon as the story leaked, however, the chance of the surviving members of the biggest band ever getting back together was quietly abandoned. But the rumours persisted.

With the line-up starting to coalesce, the BBC agreed to cover the event, clearing their schedules to run the 16-hour concert in its entirety on TV (in mono) and on radio (in stereo). The project was given to the late Mike Appleton, producer of *[The Old Grey] Whistle Test* since 1971. 'I didn't realise, to be honest, what it was it was going to become', Appleton told author Jeff Evans. 'It was a bit like a snowball going down a mountainside, getting bigger and bigger as it went along. It happened so quickly.'

The BBC's considerable outside broadcast team was engaged. Richard Skinner, Mark Ellen, Andy Kershaw and David Hepworth were tapped up to present. Reporters on the day included Janice Long, Paul Gambaccini, Andy Batten Foster (backstage) and Steve Blacknell (at Heathrow). Andy Peebles and Tommy Vance introduced the bands as they came on stage.

Andy Zweck: 'When the BBC turned up with a running schedule, we thought, "Here are some blokes who know what they're doing." Then, we saw the running order and just laughed. It was down to the minute. Down to the second.'

That a niche-market late-night music show would produce the biggest television event of all time was not lost on presenter Mark Ellen, as detailed in *Rock Stars Stole My Life!: A Big Bad Love Affair With Music* (2014):

> 'What do you think?' I asked Trevor Dann.
> 'I think', he said, scratching his baseball cap, 'that it's like getting Radio Cambridge to cover the election. But who knows? We might pull it off.'

ABC scheduled a three-hour prime time slot and MTV covered most of the rest of the US concert. 'The people at home [in the US] were raped by television', wrote Bill Graham:

> The consciousness of MTV was completely out of keeping with what Live Aid was all about. Sharing and letting go of the profit motive for one day. They were no different than the T-shirt bootleggers who worked on the streets outside of JFK Stadium. ABC butchered some of the acts because it was time for them to cut away for commercials. They didn't show the Crosby, Stills, Nash And Young reunion or the Led Zeppelin set. MTV were a

> bunch of pricks. They trivialised everything. They went for the 15-year-olds. Unfortunately, that day, not only 15-year-olds were watching.

Harvey Goldsmith: 'The day before the concert, I went out and bought 20 or 30 very large clocks and just stuck them everywhere. I sent notes around to every single act saying, I don't care what time you go on; I only care what time you come off.' Running orders with show times to the minute were displayed with the slogan, 'Kill time and you murder success'.

Midge Ure: 'Each artist had exactly 18 minutes on stage, which meant you could do four four-minute songs if you were brilliantly tight, or three five-minute songs and get off early. There was a traffic light system at the side of the stage. The stage manager warned us, "If you see the lights go from green to amber, you've got one minute left. You won't see it turn red because that is when the power goes." The fear of being stranded in front of millions of people while the power went off was enough to keep everybody absolutely on time.'

In the small hours, as the day began, Bob Geldof lay awake, his mind turning 'like an overheating engine'.

> 'Fuck me, I'm nervous', I said to Paula. For all that I was about to appear before two billion people all over the world, it did not cross my mind to wear anything other than the clothes I had automatically climbed into every morning that week. The show was not due to start for four hours, but already, through the open windows on this hot summer's morning, I could hear television sets tuned in, ready for the concert all along the street.

He memorably recalled that he felf 'like a swimmer standing on the top board, looking at the water below. It was a long way down.'

As the day began, and as crowds of punters who had queued all night for prime spots started to buzz with excitement, presenter Mark Ellen's taxi drew up outside his house in Chiswick. The ever-bluff Andy Kershaw was already installed therein. 'Mark, Mark!' Kershaw shouted, waking the street. 'Have you got your brown trousers on?'

London: 12:00 noon BST/07:00 EDT – The Regimental Band Of The Coldstream Guards

Introduced by Tommy Vance
'Royal Salute' – Official releases: digital download/DVD
'God Save The Queen'

Here is the correct answer to that old pub quiz question: 'Who performed first at Live Aid?'. Answer: the eight members of the Regimental Band Of The Coldstream Guards who played the 'Royale Salute' as Charles and Diana, the Prince and Princess of Wales, took their seats in the Royal Box alongside Bob Geldof, Elton John (and wife Renate Blauel), George Michael, Howard Jones, Nik Kershaw, David Bowie and members of Queen and The Who. Two-year-old William and nine-month-old Harry did not attend.

The BBC's broadcast from Wembley was presented by Richard Skinner – it's his voice you can hear saying, 'It's 12 noon in London, 7 am in Philadelphia, and around the world, it's time for Live Aid' – along with *Whistle Test*'s Andy Kershaw and David Hepworth. Their co-presenter, Mark Ellen, was also in attendance. Ellen later wrote: 'What rolled out for the next 16 hours had a hazy, dream-like quality, as if I couldn't quite believe it was happening, an event with all the shambling hallmarks of a village fete wrestling with the mounting news that the entire universe was apparently watching and dialling in to take part. There was a quaintness about it, a sense of Englishness, of politeness, of stunned and excitable courtesy.'

London: 12:01 BST/07:01 EDT – Status Quo

Introduced by Tommy Vance
'Rockin' All Over The World' (Fogerty) – Official releases: digital download/DVD/YouTube
'Caroline' (Rossi/Young) – Official releases: digital download/DVD/YouTube
'Don't Waste My Time' (Rossi/Young) – Official releases: digital download/YouTube

On to the stage come four skinny gents in their mid-thirties. It's Status Quo, who had enjoyed more than 20 top 20 hits in the UK over the previous 17 years but had seemingly thrown in the towel after their three-month *End Of The Road* tour between April and July 1984.

The choice of band and song was specific: 'Rocking All Over The World' was the theme of the entire global event.

'Geldof was asking if we'd open up a Band Aid-themed live concert he was organising', Rossi wrote in his memoirs:

> I admit I wasn't too sure about agreeing to Geldof's latest idea. It was one thing to organise a single day in a recording studio, where everybody – including all the artists, roadies, the studio and the video crew – gave their time for free, but a day-long concert at Wembley Stadium? That required a much greater leap of imagination – and an even greater organisational skill. I loved Bob for what he was trying to accomplish. I just wasn't sure if he was going to be able to accomplish something like that. At first, we had told Bob, 'But we're not really a band anymore. We haven't even been in the same room for a year.' Typical Bob, he just yelled back at me: 'It doesn't matter a fuck! Just get back together for the day. It doesn't matter what you sound like as long as you're there!'

'If you were to have chosen artists who best personified 1985,' writes Dylan Jones, summing up the state of pop at the halfway point of the 1980s, 'you wouldn't have chosen Status Quo. The Smiths, yes, or Prince, The Jesus And Mary Chain, Prefab Sprout, Cameo, Trouble Funk or Bruce Springsteen. But not a bunch of long-haired, denim-clad rockers whose musical offerings appeared to impress in ever-decreasing circles. It was often joked that Status Quo were perfectly named as everything they did sounded the same; but for Live Aid, though, they were perfect.'

The band met up at guitarist Rick Parfitt's local pub in Battersea and flew to Wembley by helicopter. Well, to a nearby cricket ground that was acting as a drop-off point. 'The buzz wasn't just confined to that huge Wembley Stadium crowd of over 70,000,' Rossi wrote, 'it was everywhere you turned that day. The TV, radio, people on the street, everywhere and everyone was talking about it, vibing on the whole thing – and it hadn't even started yet.'

'Had it rained on 13 July 1985,' Mark Ellen suggests, 'it would have dampened more than the charity phone appeal: it would have been the worst possible advert for the rebirth of rock. But the sight of the packed and ecstatic Wembley and the blue sky above convinced a load of hotdog-munching 30-somethings watching telly at home that the old guard could still deliver, the young guard were more important than they'd imagined and that maybe it was time to start going to gigs and buying music again. Those daunting stadiums didn't look so bad after all.'

Francis Rossi: 'Credit where it's due, it was Mike Appleton, then producer of *The Old Grey Whistle Test* and the guy who was organising the BBC's live coverage that day, who had been absolutely adamant that we should open with 'Rockin' All Over The World'. I know Bob has since usually claimed it was he who came up with that idea, and for all I know, he may well have. But that's not how I remember it. I just know Mike Appleton virtually threatened us with termination with extreme prejudice if we didn't do it. And, of course, Mike was absolutely spot-on.'

Rossi, in jeans, waistcoat and ponytail, chirrups, 'Hello! Are you all right?' The 72,000-strong Wembley crowd asset that they are indeed. A trill of boogie-woogie piano heralds Live Aid's opening band. 'Here we are and here we go…'

Famously, 'Rockin' All Over The World' was not a Quo original, having been written by John Fogerty for his self-titled 1975 album. The arrangement is 100% Status Quo, replacing Fogerty's super-charged, county-rock twanging with a four-to-the-floor shuffle, barrelhouse piano and chanted vocals. The Live Aid performance is clearly under-rehearsed and, frankly, rusty. Rossi takes half of the song to warm up his vocals. Nevertheless, the song is carried by muscle memory and sheer goodwill. It was the ideal show-opener.

The crowd-pleasing 'Caroline' keeps the momentum up. It's tight and fun, simple and effective. They close with 'Don't Waste My Time', the shuffling opening song from their breakthrough 1972 album *Piledriver*. Despite never being released as a single and having three long guitar solos, this is such a quintessential Status Quo song that it seems perfectly at home here.

Francis Rossi:

> With a large audience like that, you do usually get a good vibe, but there was something totally unique and I'm not sure I've ever felt it since. They weren't just people paying to see a show; they were part of it. There was such a euphoric feeling in that arena. It went in such a flash. I remember I got my face burnt because the sun was hitting the stage. It was a scorching day, a perfect day. We came off stage and got pissed real quick. I just hung about for the rest of the day. I think we'd been off a while when Bob came up and said, 'Fucking hell, apparently, there are two billion people watching.' I thought, 'I'm glad you didn't tell me that before.'

'Status Quo ... put a smile on the faces of 72,000 people', wrote Dylan Jones. 'So successful was their performance that it encouraged the band to question their decision to retire. It also helped focus the minds of everyone else who was going to perform that day. The bar had been set and the bar was high.'

Interviewed backstage, Rossi and Parfitt admitted that they would have liked to play longer. Bob Geldof hears this and mutters, 'You can fuck off home now; you're finished, right?' Parfitt went back to his local, where he spent the day watching the show on TV and drinking before returning for the finale. Rossi headed for the VIP enclosure. 'Freddie Mercury treated me to a bear hug that nearly broke my ribs,' he wrote, 'then picked me up and swung me around like a rag doll. I remember thinking: if Freddie decides to shag me now, there will be nothing I can do about it. He was so strong.'

Mercury had no intention of wasting his charms on the likes of Rossi.

The band's raised profile enabled them to regroup later that year and achieve renewed success with their album *In The Army Now* in 1986.

Founding guitarist Rick Parfitt died in 2016. Rossi is still rocking all over the world with Status Quo.

London: 12:19 BST/07:19 EDT – The Style Council

Introduced by Tommy Vance
'You're The Best Thing' (Weller) – Official releases: digital download/YouTube
'Big Boss Groove' (Weller) – Official releases: digital download/YouTube
'Internationalists' (Talbot/Weller) – Official releases: digital download/DVD/YouTube
'Walls Come Tumbling Down!' (Weller) – Official releases: digital download/DVD/YouTube

By mid-1985, 26-year-old Paul Weller was already working through phase two of his long career. His band, The Jam, had enjoyed considerable success from their first single, 'In The City', in spring 1977 to their last, 'Beat Surrender', at the end of 1982. They achieved 18 hits in total, including four number ones. Weller split The Jam after a final UK tour in December 1982.

Early the following year, he announced the formation of a new band, The Style Council, with keyboard player Mick Talbot, formerly of The Merton Parkas, who scraped the top 40 in 1979 with 'You Need Wheels'. The Style Council signalled a change in musical direction from the aggressive guitar-based songs of The Jam to a more soul-influenced, sometimes funky percussion, vocal and keyboard sound. *Our Favourite Shop,* the band's second album, entered the UK charts at number one the month before Live Aid.

With the crowd at Wembley stoked by Status Quo, there was a noticeable drop in energy for The Style Council's first song, 'You're The Best Thing', their sixth single from the previous summer. It goes on a tad too long and some of the crowd start to lose interest. Weller and his bandmates persist with the driving B-side 'Big Boss Groove'. It's a misstep; in front of their biggest crowd and a huge TV audience, it might have been wiser to stick to familiar songs. The angry album track 'Internationalists', despite the killer bassline by Camille Hinds, further disenfranchises the viewer.

Their set ends with a frantic and appealingly raw version of their most recent top tenner, the up-tempo 'Walls Come Tumbling Down!', which spotlights co-lead singer and future Mrs Weller DC Lee. It's a mesmerising end to a set that started well, dipped for a while, but built to a brilliant conclusion.

Weller disbanded The Style Council in 1989 and, since then, has enjoyed a long and varied solo career.

London: 12:44 BST/07:44 EDT – The Boomtown Rats

Introduced by Tommy Vance
'I Don't Like Mondays' (Geldof/Fingers) – Official releases: digital download/DVD/YouTube
'Drag Me Down' (Geldof) – Official releases: digital download/DVD/YouTube
'Rat Trap' (Geldof) – Official releases: digital download/YouTube

The Boomtown Rats enjoyed their biggest successes between 1977 and 1980 with nine top 20 singles, including two number ones, both of which they performed at Live Aid. Five years after 'Banana Republic', it seems unlikely that the band should have appeared at all. Of course, frontman and vocalist Bob Geldof deserved centre stage on this day. 'Before us was a mass of faces which moved like corn in the wind', Geldof recalled. 'They stretched across the floor of the stadium and up into the stands in all directions before me. It was the biggest crowd I had ever seen. And that was but the symbol of the vast audience we were addressing. I turned to Fingers as he walked to his keyboard. "Fuck me", I mouthed slowly in awed terror at the noise and the size as I peeled off my jacket.'

The opening 'I Don't Like Mondays', a four-week UK number one in 1979, has an unusual lyric. It recounts how 16-year-old Brenda Ann Spencer shot at children in a school playground in San Diego, killing two adults and injuring eight children and a police officer. When asked for her motive, she simply admitted, 'I don't like Mondays'.

The subject matter, cascading piano and intelligent lyrics might not have suited a massive outdoor show, but the 'tell me why' chorus gave the crowd a chance to sing along. Geldof's voice is passionate and fully committed. After two verses and two sing-along choruses, Geldof circles the stage like a caged lion as the middle eight provides an unexpected, historic moment.

> And all the playing's stopped in the playground now
> She wants to play with the toys a while
> And school's out early and soon we be learning
> And the lesson today is how to die

Geldof stands motionless, fist lifted. 'When I got to that line,' he wrote, 'there was no doubting the power that it carried. The song was brought to a halt by the massive roar of the crowd. The audience fell into a massive breathing quietness. 'Please understand', I willed that giant throng. I pushed my will through those wires. 'Please understand', up to the satellites and down to the aerials and into the living rooms of the world. Quiet. I could hear the rustle of the quiet summer breeze. Quiet as I looked right to left, down the long stadium, trying to see every face. And above me, the sky was a clear cloudless blue.'

Those lyrics, written in response to a different tragedy in a different continent, now had a powerful, unexpected resonance. Even today, re-watching it on YouTube, it's a goosebump-inducing instant in time. 'Dare I say it,' Gary Kemp of Spandau Ballet told the *Guardian,* 'it was evangelical, that moment when Geldof stopped 'I Don't Like Mondays' and raised his fist in the air. He was a sort of statesman. You would follow him. He just has a huge charisma; he'd make a frightening politician.'

Bob Geldof: 'It was only when I walked on stage with the band that the romance of it and the hugeness of it got to me. That moment when time became elastic; I stood there for hours and my hand just stayed in mid-air. Every person I had ever met in my life was probably watching.'

It would be difficult for any band to follow such a moment: 'the best day of my life', as Geldof says from the Wembley stage. The minor hit single 'Drag Me Down' from 1984 has, however, energy and passion, driven by parping horns and Geldof's unbound charisma.

The invigorating, exhilarating 'Rat Trap', another of Geldof's long, complex, intelligent, articulate songs, takes its hook from a blast of Springsteen-esque saxophone. It was the Rats' first number one in autumn 1978, replacing the interminable 'Summer Nights' from *Grease.* Sadly, this performance is marred by a failed microphone after 'Billy take a walk with me'. This rendered most of Geldof's lead vocals inaudible. Horror-struck, he breathlessly pumps out the rest of this very wordy song, but no one can hear him sing. For this reason, presumably, 'Rat Trap' is not included on the Live Aid DVD. Watch the official YouTube version released in 2018: Bob's vocals are restored, presumably flown in from a different, contemporary live version.

The Boomtown Rats disbanded after a concert in Dublin in May 1986. They reformed in 2013 and released a new album, *Citizens Of Boomtown,* in 2020, their first since the Live Aid concert.

Geldof, more than anyone, deserved this moment, his moment: a performance that changed his life and saved many others.

London: 13:01 BST/08:01 EDT – Adam Ant

Introduced by Harvey Goldsmith
'Vive Le Rock' (Ant/Pirroni) – Official releases: digital download/DVD/YouTube

Legend has it that 'Vive Le Rock' was the only song to drop down the charts after the artist's Live Aid performance. That's unfair and inaccurate. Adam Ant's seventh solo single, admittedly his lowest-charting effort to date, entered the UK charts on the day of the Live Aid concert on 13 July 1985 at number 64, rising to number 50 the following week.

One can understand the commercial decision behind this choice of song, but as an artistic showcase of Ant's eight top five singles (and three number ones,) this was a bullish, flawed choice. Ant gives it some oomph, but it's a clichéd and rather tired track.

Ant, born Stuart Goddard, would achieve one further top 20 hit with 'Room At The Top' in 1990. After well-documented mental health problems and a suspended sentence for affray, he returned to music in 2010 and has completed several tours, as well as recording two albums.

He has a tattoo which reads: 'Experience is the name everyone gives to their mistakes'.

Sydney: 13:05 BST/08:05 EDT/22:05 AEST – INXS

'What You Need' (INXS) – Official releases: digital download/DVD
'Don't Change' (INXS) – Official releases: digital download/DVD

The first satellite link-up would be with the Sydney Entertainment Centre, where a ten-hour Oz For Africa concert had seen 17 bands performing some of their best-known hits.

Mental As Anything, Men At Work and The Little River Band preceded headliners INXS, whose songs 'What You Need', their next single in Australia and a top five US hit the following year, and 'Don't Change' formed part of the global broadcast.

Already huge in Australia, worldwide success would follow this important exposure. Their next album *Listen Like Thieves* would be the band's first high-charting collection in the US and was followed by the top ten albums *Kick* and *X*. INXS had four top ten albums in the UK between 1987 and 1994.

On the morning of 22 November 1997, their magnetic singer Michael Hutchence, aged 37, was found dead in Room 524 at the Ritz-Carlton hotel in Double Bay, Sydney.

Although the BBC chose only to broadcast these two songs by INXS, ABC viewers were treated to 'Maria' and 'Overkill' by Men At Work and 'Don't Blame Me' and 'Night Owl' by Little River Band on either side of Ultravox's set from Wembley.

London: 13:17 BST/08:17 EDT – Ultravox

'Reap The Wild Wind' (Cann/Cross/Currie/Ure) – Official releases: digital download/YouTube
'Dancing With Tears In My Eyes' (Cann/Cross/Currie/Ure) – Official releases: digital download/DVD/YouTube
'One Small Day' (Cann/Cross/Currie/Ure) – Official releases: digital download/YouTube
'Vienna' (Cann/Cross/Currie/Ure) – Official releases: digital download/DVD/YouTube

> Terror. That was my overriding emotion, sheer toe-curling fear. It was a boiling hot Saturday in July and I faced a sea of faces and bodies stretching far and away into the Wembley stands. This was uncharted territory. Nobody, not Bowie, not Queen, certainly not me, had ever done anything like this before. This was the biggest show I was ever going to do.
> Midge Ure, *If I Was,* 2004

Ultravox were a band of two halves.

From 1974 until 1979, with singer John Foxx and with an exclamation point in their band name, they released three well-regarded but low-selling albums on Island Records. The band were dropped by their record company after an attempt to market the band in the United States failed to generate sales. Foxx, guitarist Robin Simon and the exclamation point left the band shortly thereafter.

It looked as though Ultravox had fizzled out. But keyboard player Billie Currie had worked with Scottish singer and songwriter Midge Ure, formerly of Silk and Rich Kids, as part of Visage in 1978. Ure signed up and revitalised Ultravox, who scored four top ten albums and ten top 20 singles in the UK between 1980 and 1984. US success continued to elude them, and by the time of their Live Aid performance, they had enjoyed their last big hit, 'Love's Great Adventure'.

Their highest-placed American single 'Reap The Wild Wind' opens their well-received Live Aid set, Ure's mirrored sunglasses reflecting the massive crowd. The ankle-length raincoat might have been an unwise choice. Their huge 1984 hit 'Dancing With Tears In My Eyes' is flawed by Ure's ever-so-flat electric guitar, but you can't fault his commitment and skills as a vocalist. Ure stretches his guitar-playing in the up-tempo 'One Small Day'. Their set ends with a brilliant rendition of the classic 'Vienna', one of the flagship British pop songs of the 1980s.

Ure wrote:

> After Ultravox performed, I was sitting backstage chatting with [Rick] Parfitt and [Francis] Rossi when I saw Freddie Mercury. I'd met all the rest of Queen, but Freddie was the invisible man: I'd never got near him. I

> went over and said, 'Hi, how are you doing?' and shook hands with him. He wouldn't let go of my hand. After he'd been holding my hand for two minutes, he said, 'Tell me, you're that lovely boy from Boomtown Rats, aren't you?' 'No', I gasped, 'I'm the lovely boy from Ultravox…' Rossi and Parfitt were pissing themselves and I was breaking out in a cold sweat. This flamboyant, gay rock god was hanging onto my hand and not letting it go while I stuttered, 'I've just got to go and talk to my girlfriend. Ooh, look. She's right over there.'

Ultravox took a break after Live Aid. Ure commenced a solo career and hit number one with 'If I Was' later in 1985. Ultravox reconvened for *U-Vox* in 1986, but despite shipping gold, sales were a disappointment and they split in 1987. The band's best-known line-up of Currie, Ure, bassist Chris Cross and drummer Warren Cann reformed in 2008 and released a new studio album in 2012. Their last shows together were in 2013.

Tokyo: 13:34 BST/08:34 EDT/21:34 JST – Loudness, Off Course, Takako Shirai, Eikichi Yazawa, Motoharu Sano, Meiko Nakahara

Loudness – 'Gotta Fight' (Takasaki/Niihara)
Off Course – 'Endless Nights' (Goodrum/Oda)
Takako Shirai – 'Foolish War' (Shirai)
Eikichi Yazawa – 'Take It Time' (Yazawa/Chiaki)
Motoharu Sano – 'Shame' (Sano)
Meiko Nakahara – 'Ro-Ro-Ro-Russian Roulette' (Nakahara)

This ten-minute segment offers excerpts from six songs from Japan's Live Aid concert, which had taken place earlier that day.

Loudness are a kind of Japanese Kiss. Off Course sing an earnest and rather limp ballad which suffered from a drop in the satellite link after about 30 seconds, forcing presenter Richard Skinner to improvise. Takako Shirai channels American AOR, as does Eikichi Yazawa, one of Japan's longest-established musical stars. Motoharu Sano's 'Shame' is perhaps best skipped over – the sentiment is welcome, but the delivery is woeful. Finally, Meiko Nakahara squeaks through the high-energy 'Ro-Ro-Ro-Russian Roulette'. This final song was not included in the BBC's coverage.

The full, uninterrupted performances of all of the Japanese contributors can be seen on YouTube.

London: 13:46 BST/08:46 EDT – Spandau Ballet

Introduced by Andy Peebles
'Only When You Leave' (G. Kemp) – Official releases: digital download/DVD/YouTube
'Virgin' (G. Kemp) – Official releases: digital download/YouTube
'True' (G. Kemp) – Official releases: digital download/DVD/YouTube

Spandau Ballet achieved consistent success between 1980 and 1986, initially with dance/funk songs such as 'To Cut A Long Story Short' and 'Chant No. 1'. They switched to a slick pop sound with their 1983 album *True* and the massive worldwide hit of the same name. Fronted by smooth-voiced Tony Hadley, the band were formed as early as 1976 by guitarist and former child actor Gary Kemp. His bass player brother Martin was added in 1978.

Their 1984-1985 tour was the group's biggest to date, spanning the UK, Ireland, Europe, the US, Japan, Australia and New Zealand. Saxophonist Steve Norman tore the anterior cruciate ligament in his knee just three dates into their American tour in April 1985. The rest of the tour was cancelled, as was a planned six-week tour of the US supporting The Power Station. Live Aid, therefore, provided some recompense.

Both Kemp brothers wrote about their experiences at Live Aid in their memoirs *I Know This Much* and *True*. Martin, though, oddly dates the event to 7 July.

Martin: 'We catch the helicopter to Wembley Stadium, where 70,000 people would be crammed onto the sacred turf to watch this huge piece of rock 'n' roll history happen before their eyes.'

Gary: 'Drawing our heads into our shoulders, we make that familiar little crouched run – pointless, but visually necessary when leaving any chopper – while enough hairspray to sear a hole in the ozone layer keeps the mullets perfectly intact.'

Martin: 'Wembley ... was buzzing with excitement. Everyone from the cleaners to the stars were hyped up and ready to rock. There were several small portable cabins backstage that were being used as makeshift dressing rooms and a small piece of astroturf had been laid down between them, with a bar at the far end giving away free water and Coca-Cola. I stood for a while and spoke to Rick from Status Quo ... he was flying with adrenaline and had a permanent smile spread across his pink face.'

Gary:

> A cordon of Winnebagos, managers and minders try to defend their stars, who seem far happier in the open air, hugging and air-kissing each other, their lanyards swinging congenially in the sun. Shades, carefully fashioned stubble, Day-Glo jackets (with Miami Vice-style half-mast sleeves), flapping silk shirts and career-shortening shoulder pads proliferate and roam in packs. Janice Long, the ordinary lass of Radio 1, is pulling some of them towards

her microphone, which is replete with a red foam knob in an attempt to make it chummy. As soon as they're in front of it, their voices change: 'Well, it's really important that we all remember what today's about, Janice.' 'Of course. Will you be doing your new single?'

Martin: 'I couldn't wait to get out there in the sunshine with the boys and play our three songs. 1.47 pm. It was our turn.'

Gary: 'We were called. Pumped, we were escorted towards the stage, me in shades and a Flaming June shirt. We hovered near the steps, enjoying the familiar, self-regarding vanity of the moment. Then, the mid-Atlantic voice of a Radio 1 DJ came over the speakers: "And now, will you welcome onstage here at Wembley, Spandau Ballet!" And they did. In truth, they were cheering themselves. The whole world was cheering what it was doing.'

Tight after many months of touring, they kick off their short set with 'Only When You Leave', the opening song from their fourth album *Parade* and their eighth top ten hit. Tony Hadley's clear, bright vocals cut through a muddy mix. It was mischievous of Spandau Ballet to perform an unreleased song at Live Aid. The pumping 'Virgin' would be included on *Through The Barricades* in 1987, but this was a brazen addition to their set, especially when they had a bagful of hit singles to go at. They finished with, what else, 'True'. Hadley sings impeccably. 'You know this,' he says. 'I want you to sing along, alright?' The crowd does as he asks.

After the Live Aid set, Gary Kemp was brought down to earth. 'I went up through the stadium and found Mum and Dad in their seats near the royal box. "Hello, boy. You were brilliant. Well done." "Thanks, Dad." "Shame, though. Charles and Di left just before you came on." "Oh. Right."'

Later in the day Gary met one of his idols back stage: David Bowie:

He was standing at the bar pretending to be an ordinary person. And suddenly, I could visualise my journey from then to here: this man was the reason I was about to take the stage in front of most of the world. He looked sensational in a slim, pastel suit. I drifted from the others and made my move. 'David? Hi. It's Gary Kemp.' His eyes flicked around at me. 'Hi.' And then returned to the guy he was with. Okay, maybe he doesn't know who I am and thinks I'm nobody; I'll qualify it: 'From Spandau Ballet…' His eyes flicked to me again; a faint grin, maybe an imperceptible nod, and then his friend spoke and I'd lost him. I mumbled something about having a good one and walked backwards while nodding like some creepy courtier.

Kemp, who said backstage afterwards that 'three numbers was like playing an entire gig', is markedly humble in his reflections of the day. He writes:

Our choice of doing a new song had been a mistake, given the number of hits we had to choose from. We could have blown the world away that

> afternoon, but our desire to promote a new album had dropped us back with the also-rans. Obviously, it was sublime charity, a passionate hymn of hope, all driven by Bob and his belief in what was right, but it was also more than raising money to save lives. On that day, ordinary people saw that their actions could affect the world and change government policy. It was a genie released into the air forever. Power to the people had finally arrived, and it had happened, surprisingly, in the eighties.

Spandau Ballet's record company, Chrysalis, capitalised on the band's performance and a period of downtime with a 15-track hits collection called *The Singles Collection* later in 1985. Disagreements with Chrysalis led to a bitter court case and a move to CBS for the band's fifth album *Through The Barricades* in 1986.

Spandau Ballet were much better musicians than their image might suggest. They split acrimoniously in 1990 but announced their reunion in March 2009, with the Live Aid lineup staying together until 2017 when Hadley quit for good.

On video footage, Gary Kemp can be seen playing a distinctive black Fender Stratocaster for 'True'. Kemp later lost this guitar. 'I played it at Live Aid', he told Dermot O'Leary on BBC Radio 2 in November 2023. 'This guitar had some importance. I had two Stratocasters, one black and one white. As the 80s went on, I started leaning towards the white one and played that a lot more. The black one went into my lock-up in about 1990. When the band got back together [in 2009], I decided to get all my guitars out, and that one wasn't there. No one could work out the last time they saw it. I was really upset about this because it was the guitar I'd played at Live Aid.' Many years later, Kemp was sent a photograph of a black Stratocaster hanging in a guitar shop in Horncastle, Lincolnshire. The guitar was labelled as 'originally Spandau Ballet, not for sale'. 'I immediately recognised it', Kemp said. 'I knew it was mine and the serial number proved it. Norman, who runs the shop, had come across it in Portobello Road market being sold on a stall by a guy who said he'd got the guitar through someone who had worked for me at one point.' Kemp agreed to donate the cost of the guitar to the local cancer trust. He took the train to Lincoln and retrieved his instrument: a small echo of Live Aid through the years.

Philadelphia: 13:51 BST/08:51 EDT – Bernard Watson

'All I Really Want To Do' (Dylan)
'Interview' (Watson)

Philadelphia is five hours behind London. But the US leg of the Live Aid concert started before 9 am, meaning that the US show kicked off around 100 minutes after the UK. Very little of the first three hours at Philadelphia was shown, retrospectively, on the live TV feeds. Sets by Joan Baez, The Four Tops, Black Sabbath, Run D.M.C., Rick Springfield, REO Speedwagon, Crosby, Stills and Nash and Judas Priest would only be enjoyed (in part) with the release of the DVD in 2004. The official attendance was 89,484.

First, though, Bernard Watson. 'Who?' you might ask. Eighteen-year-old Watson, real name David Weinstein, camped outside JFK for several days, badgering Bill Graham's office to play at the concert. This became a news story. Graham relented.

Watson is said to have performed two songs: Bob Dylan's 'All I Really Want To Do' and an original composition called 'Interview', accompanying himself on guitar and harmonica. Only 'Interview' is confirmed and this can be seen on YouTube at the time of writing. He has clearly been listening to a lot of Bob Dylan.

'One of the strings on my guitar broke,' he told the *Spokesman-Review* the following day, 'then I dropped the pick and that wasn't very professional. But I felt happy that I got a chance. I'd like to make it in this business. It was the dream of a lifetime. That's what it was.'

Philadelphia: 14:01 BST/09:01 EDT – Joan Baez

Jack Nicholson introduced by Bill Graham
Joan Baez introduced by Jack Nicholson
'Amazing Grace' (Newton) – Official releases: digital download/DVD/YouTube
'We Are The World' (Jackson/Richie)

Joan Baez had been the voice of protest for 25 years, with a commitment to political and social activism since the 1959 Newport Folk Festival.

'To pretend', Baez wrote, 'that I was less than shamelessly thrilled at the chance to open the US portion of the biggest rock 'n' roll show in the history of the world would require a sophistication I haven't got. I was given six minutes at the top, which would put me in an unfilled stadium 11 hours from prime time. I had six minutes to make some sense out of yet another 'historic moment'. I had six weeks to plan my six minutes and I had no doubt that the appropriate combination of words and songs would come to me in time. I was ecstatic.'

Her soprano voice is well-suited to the popular hymn 'Amazing Grace', an ideal song for the official start of the US Live Aid concert. Next up, Baez vocalises the chorus and a verse or two of 'We Are The World' but struggles to maintain the audience's attention.

'This is your Woodstock', she suggests. 'It's long overdue. And it's nice to know that the money out of your pockets will go to food to feed hungry children.' Bob Dylan would offer an alternative suggestion later in the day.

Baez returned to her hotel for the rest of the day to watch the TV broadcast and was particularly impressed by U2. She went back to JFK for the finale.

London: 14:07 BST/09:07 EDT – Elvis Costello

Introduced by Andy Peebles
'All You Need Is Love' (Lennon/McCartney) – Official releases: digital download/DVD/YouTube

Back in London, Elvis Costello, bearded and with a red Stratocaster, keeps it simple and sings an 'old Northern English folk song'. It's the first of the day's several covers of Beatles songs – 'All You Need Is Love'. His voice cuts clearly through the huge crowd as he reduces a verse to get straight to the chorus. He beams brightly as the crowd sing lustily.

'I took an overseas call, shortly after playing the Sydney Opera House in June 1985', Costello wrote in his engaging memoirs *Unfaithful Music And Disappearing Ink* (2015):

> Bob Geldof wanted me to sing just one song on my own after a set by Spandau Ballet and while the road crew were preparing the stage for the entrance of Nik Kershaw. It is at times like these that vanity must be laid aside. This was not about career opportunities. I honestly didn't feel I had a song of my own worth singing. Playing some song that had just scraped into the UK top 30 two years earlier or performing a hit from 1979 might have raised a cheer of recognition but would have felt trite or even seemed needy. For a moment, I thought about singing Nick Lowe's 'Peace, Love And Understanding' as a ballad, but this led me to the much better notion of singing 'All You Need Is Love'. John Lennon's song was not one that I had ever thought of performing before, so other than from singing along to the radio, I didn't have all the lyrics jammed in my head along with five hundred other songs. I wrote the keywords – 'nothing', 'nowhere' and 'no one' – on the back of my hand with a black marker [visible in a postmatch interview with the singer]. Before I knew it, I was pushed out into the sunshine in front of 70,000 sunburned people.

The song's sentiment is perfectly on point. One man, his guitar and an important message.

Philadelphia: 14:10 BST/09:10 EDT – The Hooters

Chevy Chase and Joe Piscopo introduced by Bill Graham
The Hooters introduced by Chevy Chase and Joe Piscopo
'And We Danced' (Bazilian/Hyman)
'All You Zombies' (Bazilian/Hyman)

Bob Geldof to *Rolling Stone:* 'Who the fuck are The Hooters?'

The Hooters were the biggest new band in Philadelphia in mid-1985. Songwriters Eric Bazilian and Rob Hyman had co-written 'Time After Time' for Cyndi Lauper (1984), resulting in a recording contract for their band. Their first major-release album, *Nervous Night,* would be released just five weeks before Live Aid.

The Hooters played two songs from *Nervous Night,* the minor hit single 'And We Danced' and the live favourite 'All You Zombies'. Neither song would be included on the official DVD but the coverage is available on YouTube at the time of writing. Mullets abound, but the band's musicianship is unquestionable. Their pumping opener blasts across JFK Stadium. 'All You Zombies' has a tinge of reggae. *Nervous Night* would eventually ship double platinum.

Bazilian and Hyman still perform and record with The Hooters over 40 years after forming the band. In 2007, Bob Geldof opened two shows for The Hooters in Germany. 'We did not give him a good dressing room,' Bazilian told *popdose.com*, 'but we were very nice to him, and he was sheepishly polite with us.'

Graz: 14:12 BST/09:12 EDT/15:12 CET – Austria Für Afrika

'Warum?' (Ambros/Fendrich)

Austria's equivalent of Band Aid, Austria Für Afrika was a joint project of many Austrian musicians. The song 'Warum?' (or 'Why?') was written by Wolfgang Ambros and Rainhard Fendrich and incorporates elements of Ethiopian folk music. It reached number one in the Austrian single charts.

This performance was recorded in the city of Graz ahead of the Live Aid event and featured Opus, Wilfried, Maria Bill, Wolfgang Ambross, Stefan Eberhartinger, Hansi Djumic, Peter Cornelius, Uli Baer and others. This is surely one of the greatest moments in Austrian pop history.

London: 14:22 BST/09:22 EDT – Nik Kershaw

Introduced by Tommy Vance
'Wide Boy' (Kershaw) – Official releases: digital download/YouTube
'Don Quixote' (Kershaw) – Official releases: digital download/YouTube
'The Riddle' (Kershaw) – Official releases: digital download/YouTube
'Wouldn't It Be Good' (Kershaw) – Official releases: digital download/DVD/YouTube

Nik Kershaw is an anomaly. A skilled guitarist and songwriter, he would be marketed by his record company as a synth-pop heartthrob to the teenage market. Subsequently, he was one of the biggest-selling UK solo artists between 1984 and 1985, even though, at 27, he was a little older than his contemporaries.

'At 22 minutes past two, Kershaw followed Costello onto the stage for one of the least prepossessing performances of the day', writes Dylan Jones. 'He may have attempted passion and depth in his songs, but his sedulousness was agony to watch. Nik Kershaw was far too tentative to be a proper pop star.' 'Not a blood relative', snarked presenter Andy Kershaw as he introduced his part-namesake.

Forty years later, we can watch and listen without prejudice. Kershaw is excellent, though initially clearly tense. He sang four top ten hits at Live Aid: his two most recent hit singles, 'Wide Boy' and 'The Riddle', his next release (and last top tenner), 'Don Quixote', and his first big hit, 'Wouldn't It Be Good'. The latter was Kershaw's only US chart entry.

Kershaw certainly looks nervous and he and his band kick off with 'Wide Boy', a lightweight, languid pop tune with a fluent heavy metal guitar solo in the middle. The funky 'Don Quixote' picks up the pace as Kershaw gains confidence. The band are very tight. Kershaw smiles as the crowd clap along to the snare drum introduction of the annoyingly catchy yet musically sophisticated 'The Riddle'. He closes with the uplifting 'Wouldn't It Be Good'. It's a terrific performance of a wonderful song. The whole stadium sing along with him.

Nik Kershaw had every right to be on the stage at Live Aid. His talent as a songwriter has served him well. He has written hits for Chesney Hawkes, Let Loose, Elton John, Sia, Gary Barlow, James Blunt and Bonnie Tyler.

Philadelphia: 14:32 BST/09:32 EDT – The Four Tops

Introduced by Chevy Chase
'Shake Me, Wake Me (When It's Over)' (Holland/Dozier/Holland)
Medley: 'Bernadette' – 'It's The Same Old Song' – 'Reach Out I'll Be There' – 'I Can't Help Myself (Sugar Pie, Honey Bunch)' (Holland/Dozier/Holland)

One of the few black acts at Live Aid, The Four Tops' performance is a cypher, not available officially anywhere. In their 22nd year together, without a change in membership, the singers provided a 12-minute set of some of their best-known songs. Lead baritone Levi Stubbs' powerful voice blasts through the early start time.

Opener 'Shake Me, Wake Me (When It's Over)' dates from 1966. The Tops then deliver a thrilling medley of hits: the towering 'Bernadette' from 1967, the classic 'It's The Same Old Song' from 1965 and two number ones from 1965-1966 – 'Reach Out I'll Be There' and 'I Can't Help Myself (Sugar Pie, Honey Bunch)'.

The lack of an official release is a great shame. Alongside The Four Tops, performances from Rick Springfield, The Hooters, The Power Station, Santana, Led Zeppelin, Billy Ocean and Kool And The Gang do not feature on any of the downloads, the DVD or the official YouTube channel.

The original Four Tops stayed together for over 40 years until 1997 with the death of founding member Lawrence Payton. Obie Benson died in 2005 and Levi Stubbs in 2008. As of 2024, tenor vocalist Duke Fakir has been performing with The Four Tops for seven decades.

The Hague: 14:40 BST/09:40 EDT/15:40 CET – B.B. King

'When It All Comes Down' (Jennings/Sample)
'Why I Sing The Blues' (King/Clark) – Official releases: digital download/DVD
'Don't Answer The Door' (Johnson) – Official releases: digital download/DVD
'Rock Me Baby' (King/Josea) – Official releases: digital download/DVD

B.B. King was more than 40 years into his 72-year career when parts of his concert at the North Sea Jazz Festival in The Hague were included in the Live Aid broadcast.

After an excruciating introduction by three Dutch presenters, only the last ten seconds of 'When It All Comes Down', from King's 1978 album *Midnight Believer,* is included (completists can hear the full song from a European radio broadcast).

'Why I Sing The Blues' dates from his 1969 album *Live And Well,* recorded during King's assimilation into a rock audience. It features fearsome left-hand vibrato and segues into the burning slow blues of 'Don't Answer The Door', an R&B hit from 1966. The segment ends with 'Rock Me Baby', King's big cross-over hit from 1964. He indulges in his familiar stage patter ('how about a big hand for the ladies').

King's inclusion was a welcome addition to the varied bill.

Philadelphia: 14:45 BST/09:45 EDT – Billy Ocean

Introduced by Chevy Chase
'Caribbean Queen (No More Love On The Run)' (Ocean/Diamond)
'Loverboy' (Ocean/Diamond/Lange)

As B.B. King sang the blues in The Hague, British soul singer Billy Ocean was slotted into the JFK lineup as the stage was reset after The Four Tops' performance. Singing along to his original album tracks, Ocean does his best to gee up the crowd.

'Caribbean Queen' was the first of Ocean's three US number ones between 1984 and 1988. 'The song was released in Europe as 'European Queen' and nobody was interested in it', Ocean told the Chicago Tribune in 1985. 'When we changed the name to 'Caribbean Queen' and released it in the US, it took off and started snowballing and they started playing it in Europe. I guess it had more appeal as 'Caribbean Queen' because Europe conjures up a vision of rain and snow and cold, but Caribbean sounds like sunshine and blue skies. It's much more exotic.'

'Loverboy' was the follow-up to 'Caribbean Queen' and reached number two on the US *Billboard* Hot 100.

London: 14:53 BST/09:53 EDT – Sade

'Why Can't We Live Together' (Thomas) – Official releases: digital download/ YouTube
'Your Love Is King' (Adu/Matthewman) – Official releases: digital download/ DVD/YouTube
'Is It A Crime?' (Adu/Matthewman/Hale) – Official releases: digital download/ YouTube

British band Sade, featuring bewitching lead singer Sade Adu, won the Brit Award for Best British Album in 1985 for *Diamond Life.* Furthermore, 'Smooth Operator' had been a huge hit in the US earlier that same year.

Their first song here is a cover of a Timmy Thomas track from 1972, 'Why Can't We Live Together'. Adu is elegant, mesmerising, passionate, sexy and effortlessly cool. Bassist Paul Denman wins the prize for the shortest guitar strap of the day. The crowd give a huge cheer for 'Your Love Is King', a number six UK hit from 1984.

The band close with a smooth and jazzy 'Is It A Crime?', the opening track on their second album *Promise,* which would be released later in 1985 and would top the charts in both the UK and the US. Sade naturally hold the audience's attention despite the subtlety of the band's music in such a large venue.

Sade's exposure at Live Aid certainly contributed to their global success, as writer Mark Bego suggests in his slim biography published in 1986: 'The show was a great showcase for Sade because it introduced the group to such a huge global audience. The band's first American single, 'Hang On To Your Love', was not a hit in the States because there was no visual image of the singer. Sade's performance at the Live Aid concert helped to feed the hungry, as well as spreading awareness of the group.'

Sade's first post-Live Aid single 'The Sweetest Taboo' would give them their second top-five chart entry on *Billboard's* Hot 100. They have released a further four albums and still work together.

Philadelphia: 14:55 BST/09:55 EDT – Black Sabbath

Introduced by Chevy Chase
'Children Of The Grave' (Iommi/Osbourne/Butler/Ward)
'Iron Man' (Iommi/Osbourne/Butler/Ward)
'Paranoid' (Iommi/Osbourne/Butler/Ward) – Official releases: digital download/ DVD/YouTube

Here, we have the first big reunion of the Live Aid concerts, as Ozzy Osbourne re-joins his Black Sabbath band mates Tony Iommi, Geezer Butler and Bill Ward on stage for the first time since 1978 at 10 am on a Saturday morning. As legend has it, they arrived in Philadelphia, rehearsed and partied all night, then rocked up for the gig. 'We were all drunk when we did Live Aid,' Geezer Butler told *Kerrang!* in 1997, 'but we'd all got drunk separately.'

Osbourne explains in his memoirs:

> On the one hand, doing Live Aid was brilliant: it was for a great cause, and no one can play those old Black Sabbath songs like me, Tony, Geezer and Bill. But on the other hand, it was all a bit embarrassing. For a start, I was grossly overweight – on the video, I'm the size of a planet. Also, since I'd left the band, I'd become a celebrity in America, whereas Black Sabbath had been going in the other direction. So, I got preferential treatment, even though I hadn't asked for it. It was just stupid little things like I got a Live Aid jacket and they didn't. But it still felt awkward. And I didn't handle it with much grace because my coked-up rock star ego was out of control. But the gig went smoothly enough.

Their 13-minute performance coincided exactly with Sade's Wembley set – you couldn't ask for a bigger musical contrast.

The available footage of 'Children Of The Grave', from 1971's *Masters Of Reality,* is incomplete (very ropy audio is available to those who want every note), but we're not missing much. The monster riff of 'Iron Man' cannot hide Osbourne's flat singing. They end with their signature song 'Paranoid'. Even being charitable, the performance is shite.

Also, embarrassingly, MTV showed an advert for Black Sabbath's most recent album, the universally panned *Born Again*, which featured ex- and current Deep Purple singer Ian Gillan. Gillan, for his part, was meant to join the broadcast with the rest of Deep Purple via a satellite link-up from a show at the Hallenstadion in Zurich, Switzerland. For whatever reason, and online theories are rife, this did not happen.

Belgrade: 15:10 BST/10:10 EDT/16:10 CET – YU Rock Misija

'Za Milion Godina' (Ilić/Popović)

Back when Yugoslavia still existed as a country, their contribution was the awful 'Za Milion Godina' (or 'For A Million Years'). The singers, in order, are Oliver Mandić, Husein Hasanefendić, Marina Perazić, Jura Stublić, Slađana Milošević, Peđa D'Boy, Sead Lipovača-Zele, Bora Đorđević, Goran Bregović, Anja Rupel, Aki Rahimovski, Zorica Kondža, Željko Bebek, Igor Popović, Vlatko Stefanovski, Vlada Divljan, Srđan Šaper, Zdravko Čolić, Doris Dragović, Vesna Vrandečić, Momčilo Bajagić-Bajaga, Massimo Savić, Sergio Blažić, Mladen Vojičić-Tifa, Ivana Kuzmanović, Dejan Cukić, Snežana Mišković, Alen Islamović, Neriman Mahmut-Nera, Ljubomir Ninković and Zoran Predin. Although we recognise no one here, we can have a good laugh at the 1980s clothes and posturing and remember that it's all for a good cause.

The state of Yugoslavia was broken up in 1991-1992, following a long civil war, into several new self-governing republics.

Philadelphia: 15:12 BST/10:12 EDT – Run-DMC

Introduced by Joe Piscopo
'Jam Master Jay' (Mizell)
'King Of Rock' (McDaniels/Mizell/Simmons/Smith/Simmons) – Official releases: digital download/DVD/YouTube

Here, we see Run-DMC opening many doors as the only hip-hop act at Live Aid. The band was formed in Queens, New York City, in 1983 by rappers Run (Joseph Simmons) and DMC (Darryl McDaniels), with Jam Master Jay (Jason Mizell). Run-DMC. pioneered new-school hip-hop music with their albums *Run-DMC* (1984) and *King Of Rock* (1985).

MTV played only a very short section of this performance, but ABC broadcast all of it. The track 'Jam Master Jay' is a crowd-rousing introduction, with some live scratching and rapping. 'We have a whole lot of rock groups backstage tonight,' Run says, 'but we want you to know one thing…' And 'King Of Rock' blasts across Philadelphia. It shouldn't work with this crowd and this event, but it does. 'We stepped on stage at Live Aid! All the people played and the poor got paid.'

The following year, Run-DMC memorably remade 'Walk This Way' with members of Aerosmith and achieved a top ten hit single in 13 countries.

London: 15:18 BST/10:18 EDT – Sting And Phil Collins

Introduced by Noel Edmonds
'Roxanne' (Sting) – Official releases: digital download/DVD/YouTube
'Driven To Tears' (Sting) – Official releases: digital download/YouTube
'Against All Odds (Take A Look At Me Now)' (Collins) – Official releases: digital download/DVD/YouTube
'Message In A Bottle' (Sting) – Official releases: digital download/YouTube
'In The Air Tonight' (Collins) – Official releases: digital download
'Long Long Way To Go' (Collins) – Official releases: digital download
'Every Breath You Take' (Sting) – Official releases: digital download/DVD/YouTube

By mid-1985, Phil Collins was about to reach critical mass. He had achieved three number ones in the US over the previous year ('Against All Odds (Take A Look At Me Now)', 'One More Night' and 'Sussudio') and *No Jacket Required* was the best-selling album in America the week of Live Aid.

Collins initially agreed to perform solo in Philadelphia and then to fill the drum seat for his old friend Robert Plant, with whom he had toured a couple of years before. Eric Clapton asked him to sit in for his Philadelphia set. And then Sting called. 'Are you doing this Geldof concert, Phil?' 'Yeah, I am…' 'Well,' says Sting, 'do you want to do it together?'

A plan is hatched for Collins to appear in London with Sting, then to fly to New York and on to Philadelphia for the American end of the concert. Sting and Collins rehearsed together at Phil's house in West Sussex, working up 'Long Long Way To Go' from *No Jacket Required* and a delightful arrangement of Sting's most famous song, The Police's 'Every Breath You Take'.

Collins remained down-to-earth. Backstage footage shows him collecting autographs for his kids.

Sting takes to the stage at 3.18 pm to sing 'Roxanne' and 'Driven To Tears' with jazzer Branford Marsalis tooting his soprano saxophone.

Dylan Jones writes:

> If anyone personified the generic Eighties rock star, it was Sting, a good-looking, rather imperious man with a glamorous day job. He took care of himself, a little too well for most people, and had started to take his top off at every available opportunity. The Police were initially laughed at by the music press, yet when they became the biggest group in the world, thanks to a succession of amazingly well-crafted pop-reggae singles, they couldn't ignore them. It was only when Sting decided to go solo, around the time of Live Aid, that things started to go wrong, largely because a lot of people found him a little too smug for his own good.

Phil Collins has been waiting in the wings. He sits at the piano for the most high-profile performance of his career. 'Good afternoon Wembley', he chirrups, 'good afternoon Philadelphia, good afternoon the world.'

'The stage is white,' Collins writes in his memoirs, 'and it's a very sunny day, so it's blisteringly hot up there. I'm so sweaty that my finger slips off the piano key on 'Against All Odds'. It's a real clanger, and I can almost hear 80,000 people in Wembley wincing. It's the bum note that's heard around the world.'

Sting sings the old Police hit 'Message In A Bottle' with Collins looking on, then a solid performance of 'In The Air Tonight'.

To conclude, they played and sang the wholly appropriate 'Long Long Way To Go' together and an excellent version of 'Every Breath You Take', with wonderful harmonies and spiralling saxophone. 'Every Breath You Take' was only two years old at this point.

Dylan Jones: 'It was certainly Sting's signature song and was liked even by those who tended to dismiss his work as anodyne and overcooked (a combination that was something of an achievement in itself).'

It was an impressive set. Sting stuck around at Wembley for a second appearance later in the afternoon. Collins boarded a helicopter for the quick hop to Heathrow and onwards to Philadelphia.

Intriguingly, the original running order published in the event's programme lists Sting, Phil Collins and Julian Lennon in this slot. One assumes that Lennon pulled out to quash any Beatles-to-reform-with-dead-guitarist's-son rumours.

Philadelphia: 15:27 BST/10:27 EDT – Rick Springfield

Introduced by Joe Piscopo
'Love Somebody' (Springfield)
'State Of The Heart' (McCusker)
'Human Touch' (Springfield)

Rick Springfield was a seasoned performer. He released his tenth album *Tao* in spring 1985 and enjoyed much success with the single 'Jessie's Girl' and album *Working Class Dog* in 1981. He was also familiar as Dr. Noah Drake in the long-running soap *General Hospital.*

Springfield opened his Live Aid set with 'Love Somebody', his most recent top-five hit from 1984. This shows Springfield to be a pretty boy with limited talent and a tight band. He next played his current single 'State Of The Heart'. 'Human Touch', his biggest UK hit, closed his eight-minute set.

'One of rock 'n' roll's finest hours', Springfield wrote in his autobiography. 'Given the estimated 400 million viewers who tuned in across 60 countries, it's surprising the world's TV satellites didn't all spontaneously combust.'

That may be so, but the global broadcast was focused on Sting and Phil Collins in London, not on Philadelphia, so Springfield's audience was minimal beyond JFK. It's not included on any of the official releases. Late-night viewers of the BBC's broadcast would be shown 'Love Somebody' at around 10.30 pm and 'Human Touch' an hour later.

Philadelphia: 15:47 BST/10:47 EDT – REO Speedwagon

Introduced by Chevy Chase
'Can't Fight This Feeling' (Cronin) – Official releases: digital download/DVD/YouTube
'Roll With The Changes' (Cronin) – Official releases: digital download/DVD/YouTube

REO Speedwagon were 18 years into their career by the time Live Aid rolled around and this is evident in a slick two-song set. 'Can't Fight This Feeling' had been a US number one five months before Live Aid. Kevin Cronin turns in an impressive vocal performance considering it was still before 11 am, but one gets the impression that the band were on autopilot.

Choosing not to include their other number one 'Keep On Loving You', they close their short set with 'Roll With The Changes', an up-tempo older number from their 1978 album *You Can Tune A Piano, But You Can't Tuna Fish*. Lead guitarist Gary Richrath rips an impressive solo before members of The Beach Boys and their families come on stage to help sing the chorus and deliver an striking conclusion.

Not shown live on the BBC's broadcast, the band's set would be slotted between acts later in the day, with 'Can't Fight This Feeling' shown after The Cars at around 11 pm and 'Roll With The Changes' between Power Station and Thompson Twins just after midnight, London time.

Cronin still fronts REO Speedwagon almost 60 years after founding the band.

London: 15:49 BST/10:49 EDT – Howard Jones

Introduced by Andy Peebles
'Hide And Seek' (Jones) – Official releases: digital download/DVD/YouTube

British musician Howard Jones was 28 when he scored the first of his six top-ten singles with 'New Song' in 1983. His choice of 'Hide And Seek', which reached number 12 in spring 1984, was better than that of his oversized jacket and ginger mullet. 'Hide And Seek' allowed Jones to play an impressive solo piano version, somewhat eclipsing Phil Collins' tinklings on the same instrument 20 minutes beforehand. The song's hopeful message is certainly relevant to the occasion.

Jones is clearly nervous: there is a quaver in his voice and he rushes the start of the song. His confidence builds quickly, and when he asks the crowd to sing along, he is both surprised and delighted. It was one of those great moments on this special day.

Moscow: 15:55 BST/10:55 EDT/18:55 MSK – Автограф

'Golovokruzhenie' (Sitkovetsky)
'Nam Nuzhen Mir' (Olev/Berkut)

Автограф – Autograph – were Russia's leading AOR band in the 1980s. BBC and ABC viewers, as well as attendees in Philadelphia, were shown the band performing the underwhelming 'Golovokruzhenie' ('Vertigo'). Their second track, 'Nam Nuzhen Mir' ('We Need Peace'), received a wider broadcast. This is an uninspiring prog rock song.

There's no doubting the band's commitment, and one should always respect home-grown talent, but this band remains nothing more than a novelty in the wider milieu.

London: 16:08 BST/11:08 EDT – Bryan Ferry

Introduced by Andy Peebles
'Sensation' (Ferry)
'Boys And Girls' (Ferry)
'Slave To Love' (Ferry) – Official releases: digital download/DVD/YouTube
'Jealous Guy' (Lennon) – Official releases: digital download/DVD/YouTube

Bryan Ferry, not quite 40 in July 1985, has been the lead singer in Roxy Music since 1970, enjoying a parallel solo career since 1973. The first three songs in his set were taken from his current top ten album *Boys And Girls,* which spent two weeks at number one on its release in June 1985.

Ferry looks uneasy. His set is troubled by significant sound problems as instruments and vocals float in and out of the mix. 'I have terrible memories of it all going wrong', Ferry told the *Guardian* in 2004. 'I'd put together an all-star band and the set was fraught with problems. We had David Gilmour on guitar and, poor David, his guitar wasn't working for the first couple of songs. With his first hit, the drummer put his stick through the drum skin. And then my microphone wasn't working, which for a singer is a bit of a handicap. A roadie ran on with another mic, so then I was holding two mics taped together and I wasn't really sure which one to sing into. It was a great day, though.'

These are perhaps the reasons why Ferry's first two songs, 'Sensation' and 'Boys And Girls', have never been seen since the original broadcast. Either that, or they're simply too low-key for a huge, outdoor stadium concert. You can find them on YouTube.

'Slave To Love' brings things back on track – Ferry is animated. He is more subdued in his final number, John Lennon's 'Jealous Guy'. Terrific guitar solos from Chester Kamen and David Gilmour precede an unfortunate whistling episode.

Philadelphia: 16:12 BST/11:12 EDT – Crosby, Stills & Nash

'Southern Cross' (Curtis/Curtis/Stills)
'Teach Your Children' (Nash) – Official releases: digital download/DVD/YouTube
'Suite: Judy Blue Eyes' (Stills)

From Woodstock to Live Aid. Crosby, Stills & Nash were one of just four acts to play both iconic concerts: the others were Joan Baez, Santana and The Who – although strictly speaking, CSN also needed Neil Young to fully check off their remarkable double whammy. As it happens, Young was keen to reunite…

On tour in July 1985, the trio flew in from Oklahoma, where they were gigging the night before. As with the other acoustic acts at Philadelphia, their performance is badly marred by faulty on-stage monitors. They could barely hear themselves play and sing. Crosby is barely present – he was still in thrall to his druggy lifestyle and would be arrested and jailed later that year.

'Even though CSN, at that time, was still managing to tour and fill arenas,' writes the band's biographer Dave Zimmer, 'the band's future was tenuous, as Crosby's alarming drug addiction continued to be the dominant force in his life. He was more obsessed with getting high on freebase cocaine than creating music. Friends desperately tried to convince him that he was destroying himself. But nothing – not interventions, not drug treatment programs, not even grand mal seizures, the threat of prison, or death – deterred him from his free-fall descent.'

'Southern Cross' was the band's most recent top 20 single from autumn 1982. The beginning is spoiled by a decidedly amateur introduction by Kenny Loggins and Sheena Easton on the ABC coverage.

'Teach Your Children' was, as Nash says, 'most appropriate', even if Crosby's voice is shot. The crowd sing along impressively. Less appropriate is the eight-minute, multi-part 'Suite: Judy Blues Eyes', which, on this occasion, fails to ignite.

Nine hours later, CSN would return to the JFK stage.

Cologne: 16:27 BST/11:27 EDT/18:27 CET – Band Für Afrika

'Nackt Im Wind' (Niedecken/Grönemeyer)

And here we have the German equivalent of Band Aid singing 'Nackt Im Wind' ('Naked In The Wind') at an event in Cologne.

Singing in German, the artists performing here, for the record, are Herbert Grönemeyer (the song's co-writer), Wolf Maahn, Udo Lindenberg, Nena, Heinz Rudolf Kunze, Ina Deter, Peter Maffay, Hendrik 'Henni' Nachtsheim (of Rodgau Monotones), Juliane Werding, Ulla Meinecke, Herwig Mitteregger (of Spliff), Friedel Geratsch (of Geier Sturzflug), Klaus Lage, Gitte Hænning, Hans Hartz, Peter Hein, Günther Sigl (of Spider Murphy Gang) and Ulla Meinecke. There are short solos from Richard Wester (saxophone), Bernhard 'Potsch' Potschka (guitarist from Spliff), Barny Murphy (guitarist from Spider Murphy Gang) and Reinhold Heil (Spliff's keyboard player).

Enjoy the performance on YouTube, have fun spotting the German versions of Rod Stewart and John Lydon and marvel at a great selection of awful moustaches and inappropriate haircuts. It's all for a good cause.

Killing time before Paul Young's set, the BBC switched to Andy Kershaw interviewing Sting, Howard Jones and Phil Collins backstage at Wembley. Kershaw wrote later:

> I'd got fed up already of hearing all morning that Phil Collins would be performing both in London and then Philadelphia by jetting supersonically on Concorde to the States after his Wembley appearance. Just how this would improve matters for the skeletal kids of Tigray wasn't immediately apparent and the stunt, I felt, was an emblematic exposure of the true priorities of many on the day – self-satisfaction if not self-promotion. 'What are you doing here, anyway?' I turned to ask Collins, a man whom I already held responsible for bringing Assistant Branch Manager excitement to rock 'n' roll. 'Because I thought you were supposed to be on Concorde and heading for America. Will you shove off?' He glanced at his watch and I barged him out of shot, screen left. 'Go on! Don't forget your barley sugars!' To his credit, he played along with this and disappeared.

Philadelphia: 16:29 BST/11:29 EDT – Judas Priest

Introduced by Chevy Chase
'Living After Midnight' (Halford/Downing/Tipton) – Official releases: digital download/DVD/YouTube
'The Green Manalishi (With The Two-Pronged Crown)' (Green) – Official releases: digital download/DVD/YouTube
'You've Got Another Thing Comin'' (Halford/Downing/Tipton)

The successful heavy metal band Judas Priest was an unusual choice. Although never massive sellers, with just two top 20 albums to their name by 1985, they had managed seven gold (or better) certifications in the US.

'Living After Midnight' is one of the band's most popular songs, first released in 1980 and a staple on college radio. The band are tight and loud. Singer Rob Halford is impressive, although he must have been sweaty in those leather strides. 'The Green Manalishi (With The Two-Pronged Crown)' is a furious cover of an old Fleetwood Mac song, all wah-wah guitars and stirringly effortless vocals. It's silly but brilliant. They finish with the 1982 single 'You've Got Another Thing Comin'', which includes a lively crowd sing-along.

Judas Priest are still rocking.

London: 16:40 BST/11:40 EDT – Paul Young With Alison Moyet

Introduced by Andy Peebles
'Do They Know It's Christmas?' (Geldof/Ure) – Official releases: digital download/DVD/YouTube
'Come Back And Stay' (Lee) – Official releases: digital download/DVD/YouTube
'That's The Way Love Is' (with Alison Moyet) (Whitfield/Strong) – Official releases: digital download/DVD/YouTube
'Every Time You Go Away' (Hall) – Official releases: digital download/DVD/YouTube

Paul Young was an unexpected teen idol after his debut solo album became a huge hit in 1983. Young had sung with Streetband (you might remember their 1978 novelty hit 'Toast'), which morphed into the Q-Tips in 1979. Despite huge promise, a growing reputation as a top-notch live band and a high-profile tour supporting The Who in 1981, the Q-Tips were unable to convert this into record sales. They split in early 1982 when Paul Young signed a solo recording contract with CBS Records at the relatively advanced age of 26.

Young's first two singles failed to chart, but his effortless cover of Marvin Gaye's 'Wherever I Lay My Hat' reached number one in the UK Singles Chart for three weeks in the summer of 1983. Another five top-ten singles would follow ahead of Young's late afternoon spot at Live Aid.

He opened his enervating Live Aid set with a few lines from 'Do They Know It's Christmas?', which he'd contributed to the Band Aid single a few months previously. A stunning 'Come Back And Stay' is coloured by screams from the audience, proof of Young's effortless charisma and wide appeal. His superb singing voice is matched by a peerless backing band. This is one of the best performances of the day.

He brings on Alison Moyet for a duet on the Isley Brothers' 'That's The Way Love Is', taking their cue from Marvyn Gaye's slow, psychedelic soul version. 'My manager was also looking after Alison at the time,' Young told Kevin Cooper of *UK Music Reviews* in 2018, 'and he told me that, whilst Alison didn't have a band at that time, she really did want to do something on the day. So, he hatched a plot that we should do something together.'

Despite her very obvious nerves, Moyet takes the opportunity to vocally wipe the floor with Young. He can only beam. About three minutes in, Young seems to have lost his cue. He's not happy and shakes his head until Moyet throws him an impromptu 'listen to me, pretty baby', which kicks the song back into gear.

Young wisely closed with his tremendous, shimmering cover of Hall And Oates' 'Every Time You Go Away'. Already a big hit in the UK at the end of March, it would top the US single charts within two weeks of Live Aid. Just listen to Pino Palladino's bass line, which plays a counter melody all of its own. Young's vocal is flawless and his energy is infectious. Kudos also to the trio of backing singers: Jimmy Chambers, George Chandler and Tony Jackson.

All-in-all, wonderful from start to finish. He told Kevin Cooper:

> The events of the day are not clear at all. I defy anybody to remember what happened during that day because it was an unholy mess from start to finish. There were people running around, not knowing what they were doing simply because it was the very first time that anything had been done of that magnitude. I sometimes look back on it and think, 'wow, did that really happen?'. It really was madness from start to finish. It was a rush; there were no sound checks, you did your slot, you got off stage and then, ten minutes later, after I came off stage, I was sternly asked, 'can you get out of the dressing room because Queen want to come in'. It really was madness from start to finish. It was interviews, interviews and even more interviews, and then all of a sudden, it was over.

And, after five hours, it was officially time to bring in the US concert.

Right: 'Do They Know It's Christmas?' is still the second best-selling UK single of all time. (*Phonogram/Columbia*)

Left: The US response – 'We Are The World' – was not as good. (*Columbia/CBS*)

Right: The programme for the Live Aid shows.

Left: Status Quo reunite to open the Wembley concert – raw but fun.

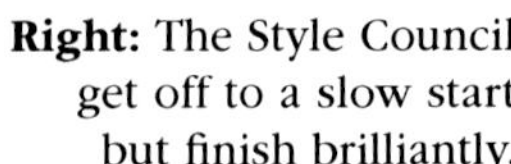

Right: The Style Council get off to a slow start but finish brilliantly.

Left: Geldof with The Boomtown Rats: 'And the lesson today is how to die.'

Right: Adam Ant sings his latest single 'Vive Le Rock'.

Left: Midge Ure, with Ultravox, singing the classic 'Vienna'.

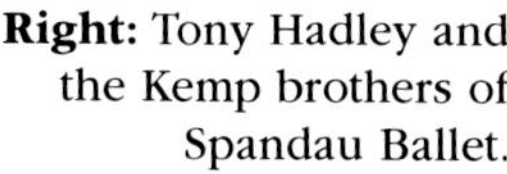

Right: Tony Hadley and the Kemp brothers of Spandau Ballet.

Left: Joan Baez kicks off the Philadelphia concert.

Right: Elvis Costello sings an 'old Northern English folk song'.

Left: Nik Kershaw. A terrific musician, unfairly packaged as a new romantic popster

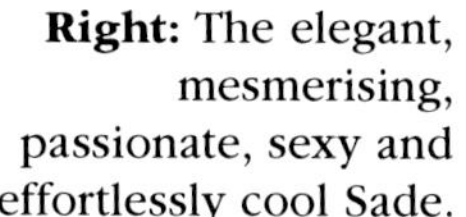

Right: The elegant, mesmerising, passionate, sexy and effortlessly cool Sade.

Left: Toni Iommi of Black Sabbath on stage at 10 am.

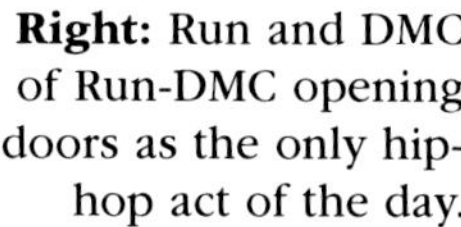

Right: Run and DMC of Run-DMC opening doors as the only hip-hop act of the day.

Left: Phil Collins and Sting – a unique pairing for Live Aid.

Right: REO Speedwagon perform a slick two-song set.

Left: Howard Jones sings 'Hide And Seek'.

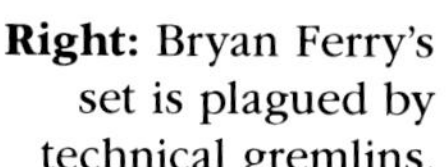

Right: Bryan Ferry's set is plagued by technical gremlins.

Left: Crosby, Stills & Nash – from Woodstock to Live Aid.

Right: Judas Priest and surfeit Marshall amplifiers.

Left: Alison Moyet joins Paul Young for 'That's The Way Love Is'.

Right: Bono and Adam Clayton of U2. The day after Live Aid, they were one of the biggest bands in the world.

Left: The Beach Boys are well-rehearsed and tight for this performance.

Right: Sting joins Dire Straits for 'Money For Nothing'.

Left: George Thorogood. The author breaks for his tea.

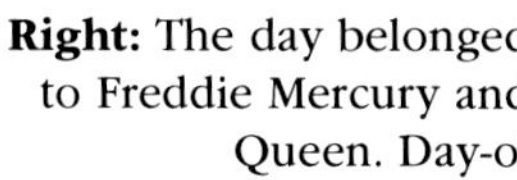

Right: The day belonged to Freddie Mercury and Queen. Day-o!

Left: Jim Kerr of Simple Minds, who flew to Philadelphia at their own expense.

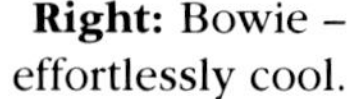

Right: Bowie – effortlessly cool.

Left: Chrissie Hynde of The Pretenders at Philadelphia.

Right: The Who's set is interrupted by a technical breakdown.

Left: Elton John on top form.

Right: Ashford And Simpson with Teddy Pendergrass – a goosebumps moment.

Left: Madonna's closing number is the interminable 'Love Makes The World Go Round'.

Right: Wembley Finale #1 – Macca croons with a quartet of famous backing singers.

Left: Wembley Finale #2 – 'It might be a bit of a cock-up, but if you're gonna cock it up, then ya may as well do it with two billion people watching yis.'

Right: Tom Petty and The Heartbreakers – tight as a drum.

Left: There was much more to Kenny Loggins than 'Footloose', a beard, great teeth, a ridiculous suit and a sculpted haircut.

Right: The Cars – flawless.

Left: Neil Young in an ill-advised sleeveless t-shirt.

Right: The Thompson Twins. 'Not identical but unsurpassable' – not really.

Left: 'By the time we got out to the stadium,' Eric Clapton wrote about Live Aid, 'I was in such a state of nerves that I was literally tongue-tied.'

Right: The bum note heard around the world.

Left: Patti LaBelle working hard.

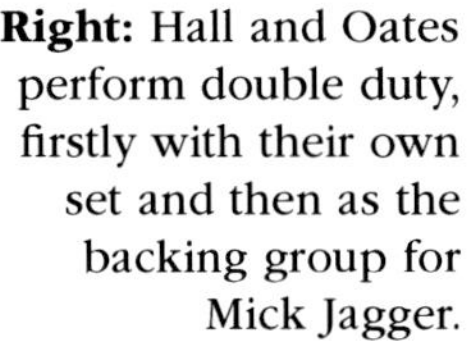

Right: Hall and Oates perform double duty, firstly with their own set and then as the backing group for Mick Jagger.

Left: Tina and Mick nose to nose.

Right: Three old fellas muck up some tunes: Wood, Dylan, Richards.

Left: Philadelphia Finale – Melissa Manchester gets her chance to shine.

Philadelphia: 17:01 BST/12:01 EDT – Bryan Adams

Introduced by Jack Nicholson
'Kids Wanna Rock' (Adams/Vallance) – Official releases: DVD/YouTube
'Summer Of '69' (Adams/Vallance) – Official releases: digital download/DVD/YouTube
'Tears Are Not Enough' (Foster/Vallance/Adams/Paiement/Hyde/Rock)
'Cuts Like A Knife' (Adams/Vallance)

Finally, it's noon in Philadelphia. This marked the start of five hours of back-and-forth between London and Philadelphia. 'The first time we went to Philadelphia', noted the BBC's editor Mike Appleton, 'we were there within 90 seconds of the time we should have been there, which is outrageous.'

The forthcoming sets from U2, Dire Straits, Queen, David Bowie, The Who and Elton John comprised an astonishing line-up for London. The Philadelphia concert provided a perfect stage for Canadian rocker Bryan Adams, who had been enjoying significant success with his fourth album *Reckless*. Adams' set opens with 'Kids Wanna Rock' from that album, a pounding statement of intent, with loud guitars and Adam's trademark throaty growl.

'Summer Of '69' was Adams' current single and a perfect choice for exploding across the JFK stadium. Adams followed this with 'Tears Are Not Enough', a mid-paced and decidedly mawkish song co-written by Adams and used for the Canadian Band Aid, Northern Lights. It's not a great song, but Adams gives it a decent attempt. This was marred by a power failure at the US stadium, which means that video is not available for this song, although decent audio exists.

'I think Bob Geldof is a saint', Adams declared ahead of his set closer, a six-minute blast of the 1983 hit 'Cuts Like A Knife'.

Live Aid was a crucial springboard for Adams. The interminable 'Everything I Do (I Do It For You)' would follow a few years later. His US success waned after 1991, but he remains a popular artist in Canada. Nine of his subsequent 11 albums would lodge in the UK top ten.

London: 17:19 BST/12:19 EDT – U2

Introduced by Tommy Vance and Jack Nicholson
'Sunday Bloody Sunday' (U2) – Official releases: digital download/DVD/YouTube
'Bad' – Official releases: digital download/DVD/YouTube

In which legends are forged.

U2 had released their fourth album *The Unforgettable Fire* in October 1984 and were 11 months through a year-long, 111-date tour to promote it. In March 1985, they were named 'Band Of The 80s' by *Rolling Stone*. Make of that what you will.

Their early evening slot on the London bill meant that U2 were the first Wembley act to perform via the transatlantic video linkup. They took to the stage following an introduction by Jack Nicholson from Philadelphia.

'Sunday Bloody Sunday', with its marching drum pattern and chiming guitars, might have been written for an outdoor concert. Its power is palpable. They look super-confident in their ability, even if Bono looks faintly ridiculous in his Cuban heels, leather strides and uber-mullet.

The second song, 'Bad', is one of the greatest moments in concert history. As the song builds dynamically, we're already six minutes in when Bono decides to dance with someone from the audience. He signalled to the yellow-jacketed security staff to pick out his chosen partner, but when she struggled to cross the barrier, he jumped into the pit himself. With the crowd roaring its approval, he hugs and slow dances with one lucky punter.

Joan Baez was watching in her Philadelphia hotel room. In her memoirs, she writes:

> I see a face I don't recognise on the screen … the singer is dressed in black and has long, slightly messy brown hair. He is streaming with sweat, and some of his hair is stuck to his cheek in road map designs, making me want to brush it back. The song is cosmic, heavenly, lilting and persistent. He calls to the audience. They call back. The singer is working his way down toward the crowd, jumping onto a narrow wooden skirt a few feet below the stage. He is gesturing to the crowd, waving someone toward him. He takes the long drop into the orchestra pit and continues his sign language invitation. Eventually, a young girl is lifted bodily and handed over the fence, which separates him from the crowd. She is simply passed over like an offering. She lands on her feet and is in his arms, and he dances with her. She is probably stagestruck and in shock, and her head is sweetly bent down. For the next few seconds, he is cradling her as they dance. I can't recall ever having seen anything like it in my life. It is an act, but it is not an act. It is a private moment, accepted by 70,000 people. All this while the percussion and hypnotic guitar continue relentlessly, lyrically, with the audience waving their arms back and forth, back and forth, a part of the ritual. There is something about his seriousness which has captivated me. Out of the hours

> of Live Aid that I saw by the end of the day, the high point was witnessing the magic of U2. They moved me as nothing else moved me. They moved me with their newness, their youth and their tenderness.

Eventually, breathless, Bono climbs back to the stage. This has taken only two minutes and 20 seconds, but Bono isn't ready to end the song, as he extemporises for a further three minutes, adding lines from 'Ruby Tuesday', 'Sympathy For The Devil' and 'Walk On The Wild Side'. These shenanigans meant that the planned performance of 'Pride (In The Name Of Love)' needed to be dropped. It was their best-known song and an opportunity for a global audience to hear it. Afterwards, Bono was mortified. Nevertheless, 'Bad' captured the spirit of Live Aid, of a global community pulling together. With millions watching, this single performance established U2 as a major act on the international stage. The following day, they were one of the biggest bands in the world.

Philadelphia: 17:39 BST/12:39 EDT – The Beach Boys

Marilyn McCoo introduced by Bill Graham
The Beach Boys introduced by Marilyn McCoo
'California Girls' (Wilson/Love)
'Help Me, Rhonda' (Wilson/Love)
'Wouldn't It Be Nice' (Wilson/Love/Asher) – Official releases: digital download/DVD/YouTube
'Good Vibrations' (Wilson/Love) – Official releases: digital download/DVD/YouTube
'Surfin' USA' (Berry/Wilson) – Official releases: digital download/DVD/YouTube

By 1985, The Beach Boys were a legacy act. They were already 25 years into their career but with just one top-ten hit in their home country since 'Good Vibrations' in 1968 ('Rock And Roll Music', 1976). However, with founder and principal songwriter Brian Wilson back on stage for the first time in many years – and with brother Carl looking snazzy in a pin-sharp suit – they are well-rehearsed and tight, with what looks like two dozen musicians on stage.

'California Girls' is dogged by a poor sound balance and Mike Love's cheesy ad-libs. This segues seamlessly into a chipper version of 'Help Me Rhonda', brilliantly sung by Al Jardine. Even if 'Wouldn't It Be Nice', featuring Brian Wilson, sounds like it will tumble base over apex at any moment, it's great to hear them harmonise and impossible not to crack a smile. Carl sings 'Good Vibrations' beautifully. This is a sublime performance of an extremely complex song despite Mike Love trying to gee up a crowd that were already totally tuned in. There, they should have ended it. The trite, throwaway 'Surfin' USA' is a needless coda.

Despite the death of Carl Wilson in 1998 (brother Dennis had died in 1983), the expulsion of Al Jardine in 1999 and the continued estrangement of Brian Wilson, The Beach Boys saga continues in casinos, state fairs and cruise ships near you.

Filling in time, BBC presenter David Hepworth asks Stuart Adamson of Big Country and comic actor Tracey Ullman whether they are looking forward to Paul McCartney playing as part of Wembley's finale.

'I keep asking people, you know,' she says, 'are *they* really gonna get up there [with Paul] … George Harrison, Ringo Starr and Julian [Lennon]. They just say, "we don't know". I bet they do know.'

'What do you think they'd play if they did that?' Hepworth asks.

'A selection of hits,' Adamson muses. 'I dunno if Julian knows any of them.'

'We don't know what's going to happen', Hepworth explains. 'We must make that clear. I think we're ready now for our next band on stage.'

London: 18:00 BST/13:00 EDT – Dire Straits With Sting

Introduced by Tommy Vance and Bill Graham
'Money For Nothing' (Knopfler/Sting) – Official releases: digital download/DVD/YouTube
'Sultans Of Swing' (Knopfler) – Official releases: digital download/DVD/YouTube

Love 'em or hate 'em, Dire Straits were massive in 1985. 'Money For Nothing' was released as a single on 28 June, the second spin-off from their fifth album *Brothers In Arms,* which was released in May and was supported by a year-long tour. As part of this, they were booked for 13 consecutive nights at the Wembley Arena between 4 and 16 July, inconveniently clashing with the Live Aid concert a short distance away. In his memoirs, bassist John Illsley writes:

> It was now being said, though never by us, that we had become the biggest band in the world and it was for this reason that we were faced with a very awkward moral dilemma. Bob Geldof was … struggling to persuade many of the big acts and artists to take part, pulling his hair out and banging phones. Bob was very keen – 'I absolutely focking insist' – that Dire Straits headlined the concert, arguing that if he got us on board, all the others would follow. The problem was that we were contracted to play the Arena the same night and all the 12,500 tickets had been sold months before. Did we let down our loyal fans, or did we fail to meet an arguably more powerful moral imperative and decline to add our voices to a global appeal aimed at alleviating widespread suffering? The talks went back and forth, and eventually, Bob had to concede that it was impossible for us to headline, so we agreed to perform in the late afternoon. After our soundcheck at the Arena, we walked across the parking lot to Wembley Stadium and went on in between U2 and Queen. Every band had different settings and the crew that day did an extraordinary job in pulling it off. On top of everything else, Live Aid was a logistical feat of the highest order. Our performance didn't let us down, but, in retrospect, I'm just very glad we came on before rather than after Queen.

The band were joined on stage by Sting, who sang backing vocals on 'Money For Nothing' with a few well-managed mistakes and the occasional fraught glance exposing zero rehearsals. This exposure, coupled with a super-tight, if slightly rushed, performance, helped the song to top the *Billboard* charts for three weeks in September.

An 11-minute version of the band's first hit single 'Sultans Of Swing' completed their set. This is their full live arrangement from 1985 and includes a smart transition into a piano part with a jazzy saxophone and some effortlessly gorgeous call and response from Mark Knopfler as they ramp back up to the full pace of the final few minutes. An 11-minute rock song with long guitar solos on BBC1 prime time? If it looks like a duck and sounds like a duck...

'Aware that we had just taken part in a great historical event,' writes John Illsley, 'it was an odd sensation when, half an hour later, we were out the rear and crossing the parking lot back to the Arena, with the security guy there hassling us for our passes. That was our tenth show at the Arena and the band were on top form, buoyed up by having just played at the biggest show on Earth.'

Philadelphia: 18:26 BST/13:26 EDT – George Thorogood And The Destroyers With Bo Diddley And Albert Collins

Introduced by George Segal
'Who Do You Love?' (McDaniel)
'The Sky Is Crying' (James) – Official releases: YouTube
'Madison Blues' (James) – Official releases: digital download/DVD/YouTube

Well, if the worldwide audience knew who Dire Straits were, then very few would recognise American blues shouters George Thorogood and the Destroyers. Then again, choosing not to play your most famous song, 'Bad To The Bone', was contrary, to say the least. Thorogood was, and remains, a constant presence on the concert circuit.

His opening song, the antique 'Who Do You Love?', featured the song's writer Bo Diddley. This was seemingly only broadcast in West Germany. Diddley's mid-song introduction lifted the mood and provided one of the few chances to see a black artist at Live Aid. Real rock 'n' roll amongst all the shoulder pads and mullets.

'The Sky Is Crying' is another vintage blues song, first recorded by Elmore James in 1959. Thorogood spanks the slide guitar, even though his vocal skills are open to question.

A thrilling, energetic 'Madison Blues', a second Elmore James song, closes the set with a spiky, if rough-and-ready, solo from second guest Albert Collins. There is so much drive in Thorogood's performance – and the crowd are duly appreciative – that we must forgive the occasional cliches on display.

The original running order shows Tears For Fears in this slot. Bob Geldof wrote the following year:

> Tears For Fears were a big band. They were number one in the States at the time of Live Aid. I asked them to do the gig very early on and they hoped to make it. A few weeks before the event, they pulled out. Their manager had 'given me his word'. I spoke to him. 'Listen, I'm not pressurizing you; it's your choice. But I think it's pathetic. After all the trouble I've been having with the Americans and now a fucking English band lets me down.' 'They've had a very hairy tour, Bob. There's a lot of internal dissent in the band. Maybe if they could use backing tracks?' 'They can hang by their bollocks from a gantry for all I care, so long as they sing live.' Their manager went back to the band and told them … that every other band would be doing their best to keep some people alive… but they were scared of not having a sound check, which was only going to be possible for the first three bands, so they came out in the press and accused me of moral blackmail. I had never spoken to them.

'I was pissed off because Bob had announced we were doing it without even asking us and it was smack in the middle of a year-long tour', Curt Smith explained to *NME* in 2022. 'It was the first week off we had. We kissed and made up with Bob and did 'Everybody Wants To Rule The World' for him [for Sport Aid] afterwards.'

London: 18:41 BST/13:41 EDT – Queen

Introduced by Griff Rhys Jones and Mel Smith
'Bohemian Rhapsody' (Mercury) – Official releases: digital download/DVD/YouTube
'Radio Ga Ga' (Taylor) – Official releases: digital download/DVD/YouTube
'Hammer To Fall' (May) – Official releases: digital download/DVD/YouTube
'Crazy Little Thing Called Love' (Mercury) – Official releases: digital download/DVD/YouTube
'We Will Rock You' (May) – Official releases: digital download/DVD/YouTube
'We Are The Champions' (Mercury) – Official releases: digital download/DVD/YouTube

Queen owned Live Aid, but they had to be pushed hard to take part. They played to an estimated 700,000 people over two nights in Rio de Janiero earlier that year: a victory lap that would give them pause as they determined their next move. Or whether there would be a next move at all. The flip side of this was playing nine gigs at the infamous Sun City gambling resort in South Africa. This was a direct violation of the United Nations' cultural boycott and led to accusations of the band supporting apartheid.

Bob Geldof recalled, in his autobiography: 'I traced Jim [Beach, Queen manager] all the way down to ... some little seaside resort that he was staying at, and I said, 'Look, for Christ's sake, you know, what's wrong with them?' Jim said, 'Oh, you know, Freddie's very sensitive.' So I said, 'Tell the old faggot it's gonna be the biggest thing that ever happened – this huge mega thing.' So, eventually, they got back and said okay, they would definitely be doing it. It was the perfect stage for Freddie. He could ponce about in front of the whole world.'

Live Aid would provide the ideal answer to the 'what next?' question hanging over Queen.

'Everyone will be trying to outdo each other, which will cause a bit of friction', said Mercury at the time. 'It makes me personally proud to be a part of it.'

Queen relished the chance to pitch themselves against other acts and spent several days rehearsing their set at the Shaw Theatre in Camden, London. They had achieved four top 20 hits over the previous year and a half. Seven of their albums were in the UK album chart in autumn 1984. Their most recent 48-date tour, taking in the UK, Belgium, Ireland, Germany, Italy, France, the Netherlands, Austria, Brazil, New Zealand, Australia, Japan and South Africa, finished in mid-May. They were road-tested and ready to prove themselves.

Using the same sets, lights, backdrops and sound system as all the other artists, the focus was entirely on the songs and the performances. 'I'm not sure what we were expecting – after all, how exciting could Queen really be?' writes Dylan Jones. 'Having never been a huge fan and never really understanding what all the fuss was about, I certainly didn't think that this was going to be the greatest stadium performance of all time.'

From the moment he came on stage, dressed in a tight white singlet so that those two billion people could pick him out, Freddie Mercury was effervescent, hyped up and ready to entertain. Freddie places himself at the piano stage right – a knowing half-grin on his face – runs through some octaves to test sound levels and counts out the ballad section of 'Bohemian Rhapsody'. The crowd at Wembley sing along from the first line.

The BBC cameraman is close enough for TV viewers to count the beads of sweat on Mercury's forehead. The first two minutes focus exclusively on Freddie Mercury. The power and control in his voice is dazzling. May's power chord ends the truncated 'Bohemian Rhapsody', and Freddie takes centre stage with his trademark mic stand as the burbling introduction to 'Radio Ga Ga' kicks in. Freddie struts, dances, nods, smiles. Here is a man in his natural element. None of it seems contrived: Freddie Mercury's charisma is palpable. The sight of Mercury, cocksure, legs apart, fist raised, encouraging the London crowd to clap to the chorus of 'Radio Ga Ga', is surely one of the defining images of the 1980s.

'I remember thinking, "oh great, they've picked it up", Brian May told *Mojo* in 1999. 'And then I thought, "this is not a Queen audience." This is a general audience who've bought tickets before they even knew we were on the bill. And they all did it. How did they know? Nobody told them to do it.'

A small skip at the end of this song shows just how keyed up Mercury was. 'Eh-oh', he sings. 'Eh-oh' is repeated by 72,000 voices. Six minutes into the greatest performance of his life, Mercury has the world in the palm of his hand. Mark Blake in *Is This the Real Life?* (2010) writes:

> From here on, the group appears invincible. Mercury teases the audience, flexing his vocal cords with some call-and-response banter before launching into 'Hammer To Fall'. A modest hit, its comic-book heavy metal is still made for stadiums such as these. A visibly more relaxed Brian May whips out the riff while Mercury joshes with the on-stage cameraman, mugging into his lens before prancing around the guitarist like a goading bull. Then, while May scrubs away, Mercury fixes the crowd with a mischievous smile and starts tugging the end of the microphone, now pointing out at crotch level. Less lusty rock star, more naughty schoolboy, the twinkle in Freddie's eye suggests that he takes none of this, including himself, seriously.

'Hammer To Fall' ends with Mercury pointing his arse at 72,000 people. A strutting 'Crazy Little Thing Called Love' – in which Brian May manages to use three different guitars in three minutes – is 'dedicated to all you beautiful people tonight'. A pounding, abbreviated 'We Will Rock You' and the inevitable 'We Are The Champions', with the Wembley crowd swaying like a living organism, close the set. A theatrical bow: 'thank you, goodnight, we love you!'

'Queen were absolutely the best band of the day', said Bob Geldof later. 'Whatever your personal taste was irrelevant. When the day came, they played the best, they had the best sound and they used their time to the full. They understood the idea exactly – that it was a global jukebox. They just went and smashed out one hit after the other. It was just unbelievable.'

Brian May: 'Looking back, I think we were all a bit over-excited, and I remember coming off and thinking it was very scrappy. But there was a lot of very good energy, too. Freddie was our secret weapon. He was able to reach out to everybody in that stadium effortlessly, and I think it was really his night.'

Live Aid would continue for another seven hours, but the day belonged to Queen.

London: 19:00 BST/14:00 EDT – Intermission

> We have a very big, special treat for you now. Two of the greatest singers of all time, for the first time ever, are going to sing on videotape one of the great classics, 'Dancing In The Streets' [sic]. Mick Jagger and David Bowie. Watch the screen!
> Chevy Chase, on stage at Philadelphia

Bowie and Jagger had originally considered a live duet, with Bowie in London and Jagger in Philadelphia. This proved to be technically impossible. 'After several attempts at working out a way to make it work, they eventually decided that this wasn't going to happen', promoter and co-organiser Harvey Goldsmith said. 'And so we all went off to a nightclub together and they spent the evening trying to outdo each other on the dance floor. Each of them was trying to attract the attention of all the girls in the club, but mostly, they were competing with each other. This gave them the idea of recording a cover of 'Dancing In The Street' to be broadcast at the Wembley event and released as a single.'

Martha And The Vandellas' 'Dancing In The Street' was first released in 1964. Bowie and Jagger recorded their vocals in a single day, 21 years later, on 29 June 1985. 'David phoned me,' guitarist Kevin Armstrong recalled, 'and said he'd been asked to do this big charity thing with Geldof, and did I want to be involved? So I went to meet them in the middle of the night in a basement in Wardour Street to do some preliminary work. It was just him and Mick Jagger in a tiny room, and we all sat down and worked out 'Dancing In The Street'. It was a pretty pedestrian version, and neither of them thought it was brilliant, but we knew we had to get it done quickly.'

They shot the very silly video through the night in London. It's lots of fun, as both singers ham it up outrageously.

Armstrong: 'We were all invited down to the video shoot in Docklands after the session to watch the pair of them camping it up for the cameras, clowning about. The dynamic between them was interesting, as there was quite a lot of banter. David knew he had to work at performing, and he had obviously worked at it psychologically as well. He was not a natural performer, whereas, with Jagger, it seemed effortless.'

'Bowie, in a long camouflage overcoat, looked the more stylish,' wrote Jagger's biographer Philip Norman, 'although Mick worked his still-tiny butt off, trumpeting his lips and dilating his eyes as ferociously as a Maori warrior. Halfway through, just to show who was still the coolest and who still didn't give a fuck, he picked a canned drink off the ground and sipped from it.'

'[Jagger] could walk in with a toothpick and make it happen,' Kevin Armstrong writes, 'whereas Bowie was much more studied. My fondest memory of David that day is the laughter. For somebody who's such an amazingly layered and sophisticated person, he could have been very intense and introverted. But there was a lot of laughter in him. A lot.'

After the video had been broadcast, the BBC coverage reverted to their presenters' studio, where David Hepworth was joined by one B. Geldof.

Hepworth: 'Now Bob, you've just taken a rather special telephone call about ten minutes ago.'

Geldof: 'Yes, we got a telephone call from Sheikh Mana al Maktoum and the Dubai government have just given us a million pounds. So, 'thank you' to the Dubai government and the al Maktoum family. The other thing is that Mick and Dave did that video specifically so that you could give something, and it's not happening enough. You know, you've gotta get on the phone and take the money out of your pocket. Don't go to the pub tonight. Please stay in and give us the money. There are people dying [slaps table] now, so [slaps table] give me the [slaps table] money! And here's the numbers…'

Hepworth: 'We're giving the addresses first, aren't we?'

Geldof: 'No, let's just… fuck the addresses, let's get the numbers…'

And thus was born the urban myth that Geldof said, 'just give me yer fookin' money…' He didn't. Mark Ellen writes:

> Had he delivered this jumble of words at five past seven on any other evening, he'd have been hauled off-air with a shepherd's crook while a long-faced colleague made a hand-wringing apology. But this was the tipping point. The tide turned. Bob Geldof had spent six months putting this show together and the world was applauding. They'd wired up TVs in their gardens, they'd lit barbecues and opened cans of lager, but not many fancied paying for it. Understandably, he'd cracked. He wasn't cautioned or reproached – in fact, no one even mentioned it. There was nothing but silent sympathy. And from that moment, the floodgates opened and the money began pouring in.

For its part, 'Dancing In The Streets' would be issued as a single five weeks after Live Aid, with all profits going to the charity. The song topped the UK singles chart for four weeks and reached number seven in the US.

Philadelphia: 19:05 BST/14:05 EDT – Simple Minds

Introduced by Joe Piscopo
'Ghostdancing' (Kerr/Burchill/MacNeil) – Official releases: digital download/DVD/YouTube
'Don't You (Forget About Me)' (Forsey/Schiff) – Official releases: digital download/DVD/YouTube
'Promised You A Miracle' (Kerr/Burchill/MacNeil/Forbes) – Official releases: YouTube

Simple Minds had been number one in the US with 'Don't You (Forget About Me)' that May. It was their biggest American hit and their first British top tenner.

In an interview with Janice Long in 2018, singer Jim Kerr explained how the band were badgered to play in Philadelphia. Kerr said:

> Live Aid came up and Geldof called us and he said, 'You've got to do Live Aid', and we said, 'Fantastic. And who's doing it?' And he told us. But he said, 'they're in Wembley, but you're not going to do it in Wembley. You're number one in America. You've got to do it in America'. So, we did it in America. And people ask, 'what do you remember of it?' When you do these festival things, you've only got 15 minutes or so; it flashes by you so quickly that it's hard for you to have a memory. But you have to think about how colossal this was. We'd never played two of the songs we were about to play live. The televised audience at that time was going to be the biggest globalised event ever. Not much pressure, then! And we're walking up to go on stage and Bill Graham walks up to us, stuck his head down in amongst us, like a bull, and he made clear, 'You mothers go one minute over 15 minutes and I'm gonna rip...' I think he did that to everyone. It was terrifying. He said, 'Who's the singer?' And I said, 'Me'. And he said, 'The presenter's going to introduce you. Go over to him. As soon as he gives you the nod, start playing.' Who's the presenter? Jack Nicholson. So, I just spent the next 13 minutes thinking, 'Jack Nicholson'. The last two minutes I spent thinking, 'Whatever made me think I should've worn these trousers?' I could feel them flapping in the wind. They would've been good for yachting. I don't know what I was thinking. But I just thought, 'wrong trousers'. That's my memory of Live Aid.

They cheekily opened their set with a new song, 'Ghostdancing', from their in-progress album *Once Upon A Time.* It's a big number and the band come across impressively, despite some hit-and-miss vocals. New bass player John Giblin, making his live debut with the band, looks utterly unfazed.

A seven-minute 'Don't You (Forget About Me)' is powerful and authoritative, even when it sounds like it might fall to pieces at any second. Kerr prowls the stage for a long call-and-response section, which lifts the crowd.

Presumably aware of Bill Graham's warning, the band leave the stage, then quickly return for a snappy version of their 1983 hit 'Promised You A Miracle'. Two minutes in, the sound feed is lost. It's an unfortunate ending to a strong performance from a band that continue to tour, releasing top-five albums as recently as 2018 and 2022.

London: 19:23 BST/14:23 EDT – David Bowie

Introduced by Andy Peebles and Chevy Chase
'TVC 15' (Bowie) – Official releases: digital download/DVD/YouTube
'Rebel Rebel' (Bowie) – Official releases: digital download/DVD/YouTube
'Modern Love' (Bowie) – Official releases: digital download/DVD/YouTube
'"Heroes"' (Bowie/Eno) – Official releases: digital download/DVD/YouTube

'TVC 15'? Really?

Bowie pulled together a scratch band for this, a rare live performance between major world tours in 1983 and 1987. In mid-1985, Bowie was in the middle of production, filming his role as Jareth, the king of the goblins, in Jim Henson's *Labyrinth*. He asked Kevin Armstrong and Matthew Seligman, with whom he'd recently worked on the *Absolute Beginners* soundtrack and the Mick Jagger duet 'Dancing In The Street', to be in his band for the event. 'We didn't have much time to prepare,' Armstrong said, 'just two days' rehearsal at Bray Studios in Berkshire, but we were ready.'

Armstrong had recorded with keyboard player Thomas Dolby on his first two albums *The Golden Age Of Wireless* (1982) and *The Flat Earth* (1984). Dolby writes in his autobiography:

> Bowie had been a huge part of my early life. I had pored over his lyrics and album covers and paid to see him in concert probably five times. When I took his phone call at Olympic Studios, I could barely talk. It was like that familiar dream when you're watching a movie on the big screen, and suddenly, the leading man turns and starts to speak to you. He was disarmingly civil and gracious. 'Oh, Thomas, would you play with me at this Live Aid thing?' he said. He sounded the perfect gentleman. The band were quickly assembled. Neil Conti from Prefab Sprout was added on drums, along with Pedro Ortiz on percussion, sax player Clare Hirst and backing singers Tessa Niles and Helena Springs – all part of the generation that had grown up idolising Bowie. We set up at a rehearsal studio in West Kensington with a list of songs he wanted us to prepare. We had a total of three evening rehearsals. He showed up after his long shooting day at Elstree had wrapped and only stuck around for a couple of hours. When he strode into the room with a slick suit and newly blond hair, he shone like a beacon of light.

It was only on the last day of rehearsals that Bowie settled on his four-song set. 'TVC 15', a minor hit single from 1976; 'Modern Love', his biggest most recent single; the classic 'Rebel Rebel', a top five hit from 1974; and the timeless '"Heroes"'. Thomas Dolby writes:

> Morning broke on the day of the Live Aid concert. It was a beautiful day. I walked along the river near my home in Fulham and everybody had their

> patio doors open. You could hear the TV commentary preamble coming out from every upstairs window. The whole city was gearing up for the event. Wembley is a distance outside central London, and because of the gridlocked traffic, I was required to make my way to Battersea Heliport by the Thames, where I was to share a helicopter to the stadium with Bowie himself. As we approached Wembley, we could see its famous twin gold towers gleaming in the distance, and I caught a glimpse of the massive crowd assembled inside the stadium. Above the stage was a giant video screen, and as we banked over the stadium, the chain-smoking Bowie was silhouetted against a massive close-up of Freddie Mercury, crooning to the heavens, reaching the climax of 'We Are The Champions'.

Bowie and Dolby were chauffeured half a mile to the stadium and almost immediately led onto the stage.

'On the day, nobody could ignore the atmosphere that Queen created, as they had just been on before us', guitarist Kevin Armstrong said. 'But... we were with David Bowie. We were going to walk on there and they were going to go nuts. And they did. By the time we hit the stage, it was probably the best part of the day, the late afternoon. I'd never felt anything like that crowd. It did really seem to be like, you know, we're here to change the world.'

Thomas Dolby tinkles the honky-tonk piano introduction to 'TVC 15', a bold and brilliant choice. Bowie smiles and struts. Within seconds, he is the coolest man on the planet. His voice has a rough edge on 'Modern Love'. The band are cooking and Bowie is energised. He takes the crowd, still pumped up by Queen, with him. Bowie's sheer presence is masterful.

Kevin Armstrong excitedly plays the iconic riff from 'Rebel Rebel'. He dances ridiculously, caught up in the moment.

'I watched Bowie from behind my keyboards,' Thomas Dolby writes, 'framed against the seething hordes as he caressed the mic stand in his rather close-cut, light blue suit, manipulating the crowd, seducing them. Even though we'd never played the songs back-to-back, the set had a great flow to it and the intensity was building.'

Bowie, sweat on his forehead, classily takes the trouble to introduce each band member as the pumping introduction to the immortal '"Heroes"' starts to build.

Kevin Armstrong: 'We were mainly running on adrenaline, but as soon as we started rocking, we went into this sort of more religious feeling, particularly when we played '"Heroes"'. Then, it was a mixture of euphoria and stage fright because '"Heroes"' doesn't actually have that many changes in it. Simple songs are sometimes the easiest to mess up because you really have to concentrate; with more complicated songs, the chord sequences keep you focused. But with '"Heroes"', you really had to know what was going on.'

Thomas Dolby:

> I was secretly dreading our finale, '"Heroes"'. Although it's a deceptively simple song, with only one or two chord changes, those are sometimes the easiest to mess up, and my synth line was very prominent. The tempo was a clear change down in gears, and as we blasted through the intro, the crowd began to raise their bare arms, waving banners and singing along with the words. I barely looked down at my fingers. I didn't have to worry about forgetting the parts because my teenage fanboy self took over and the keys seemed to play themselves. I joined in and sang the answer phrases to his lead vocal: 'I remember', 'by the Wall', 'over our heads', 'nothing could fall'. I was at one with the Wembley crowd, loving being a part of this timeless Bowie classic as if I were still 14 years old.

Armstrong: 'There are singers who have great dexterity and singers who have great character, and Bowie had the ability to fuse the two. So, I had also turned into a fanboy who was miraculously onstage with Bowie.'

Go and watch this on YouTube immediately.

As the band leave the stage, Bowie announces, 'Lest we forget why we're here. I'd like to introduce a video made by CBC Television; the subject speaks for itself. Please send your money in…'

Bowie. Genius. That's all.

London: 19:43 BST/14:43 EDT – 'Drive'

During preparation for the Live Aid concerts, Bob Geldof was interviewed by the Canadian Broadcasting Corporation. He wrote:

> At the end, they wanted to show me something. They played a video. It was a short sequence of a child, weakened by hunger, trying and trying and trying again to stand up on his little matchstick legs. They had edited it over a record. It was the Cars' 'Drive'. The juxtaposition was bizarre. The child's pitiful courage turned the poignancy of the song into a profound sadness. Who's gonna pick you up when you fall down? We can't go on saying nothing's wrong. Who's going to drive you home tonight? My eyes filled with tears and my voice caught in my throat. That video, with its two incongruous components, seemed another symbol of what Live Aid stood for. It is a beautiful song, ostensibly about love, but it is also a song about dependence, something I hadn't realised, nor indeed had the writer of the song, for when I showed him the video, he was shocked. 'I never realised', he said and broke off, too upset to continue. The artificial and, at times, indulgent world of pop was harnessed in an improbable marriage with the most basic human feelings of compassion.

David Bowie magnanimously agreed to drop one of the songs from his set to make space for the broadcast of this film, smack in the middle of the UK's prime-time TV schedule.

Various rumours have circulated about which song Bowie elected to omit. Bob Geldof's partner Paula Yates claimed, in a Channel 4 documentary in 1985, that it was 'Five Years', the apocalyptic opening track from *Ziggy Stardust And The Spiders From Mars.*

Thomas Dolby, when interviewed by journalist Steve Pafforth in 2013, said, 'David would keep changing his mind about what songs to do. He initially wanted to do his current single 'Loving The Alien', but as he got focused on what the event was, he realised that it wasn't about promoting your current single. Because he was shooting *Labyrinth,* we only had [a few] short rehearsals in the evenings, and each time, he would change his mind about what we should do. So, we only settled on the four songs that we did on the last day.'

Bowie's sacrifice ensured that the CBC film was shown to the stadium audiences in London and Philadelphia, as well as on the BBC feed to televisions around the world. ABC and MTV chose not to show the film. It remains one of the enduring moments of Live Aid.

Philadelphia: 19:41 BST/14:41 EDT – Pretenders

Introduced by Grace Slick
'Time The Avenger' (Hynde)
'Message Of Love' (Hynde)
'Stop Your Sobbing' (Davies) – Official releases: digital download/DVD/YouTube
'Back On The Chain Gang' (Hynde) – Official releases: digital download/DVD/YouTube
'Middle Of The Road' (Hynde) – Official releases: digital download/DVD/YouTube

The Pretenders formed in March 1978. By the end of 1979, they were number one with 'Brass In Pocket'. The deaths of founder members Pete Farndon (bass) and James Honeyman-Scott (guitars) could have finished the band, but they regrouped for their third album *Learning To Crawl,* which was a critical and commercial success, reaching number five on the *Billboard* 200, their highest-charting album in the US.

'Time The Avenger', a track from *Learning To Crawl,* is a robust, if unfamiliar opening. The video footage is, unfortunately, incomplete. 'Message Of Love', their first US singles chart entry, suffers from feedback but is tight and fun. Chrissie Hynde is mesmerising for the 1.57 blast of 'Stop Your Sobbing', the band's first single from 1979, a cover of an old song by The Kinks.

They close with their two biggest hits in the US so far. Firstly, the wonderful 'Back On The Chain Gang'. Hynde wrote the song as a memorial to Honeyman-Scott, who died of a drug-related heart attack in June 1982, aged 25. This is clearly a personal song for Hynde. Around 2.45, just as she sings, 'and those were the happiest days of our lives', it looks like she's about to burst into tears, but she rallies for a dynamic, emotional conclusion. Finally, the fast, powerful, rocking 'Middle Of The Road'. They sneaked in a warm-up show at the Chestnut Cabaret in the University City suburb of Philadelphia the night before Live Aid, and it shows.

Their next album, 1986's *Get Close,* included their second and last US top-ten single 'Don't Get Me Wrong'. Live Aid was founding drummer Martin Chambers' last gig with the band until 1993. But since rejoining, Hynde and Chambers, and a rotating cast of musicians, have released a further seven albums and the classic single 'I'll Stand By You'.

Their 50th anniversary as a band approaches soon.

London: 19:59 BST/14:59 EDT – The Who

Introduced by Jack Nicholson and Tommy Vance
'My Generation' (Townshend) – Official releases: YouTube
'Pinball Wizard' (Townshend)
'Love, Reign O'er Me' (Townshend) – Official releases: digital download/DVD/YouTube
'Won't Get Fooled Again' (Townshend) – Official releases: digital download/DVD/YouTube

The Who performed their final concerts in 1982. 'So that was it', wrote singer Roger Daltrey in his autobiography. 'Apart from Live Aid in 1985 – which silver-tongued Bob talked me into.' Bob Geldof approached both Daltrey and guitarist Pete Townshend about re-forming The Who for the show. Townshend was open to the idea, but Daltrey didn't want to play with drummer Kenney Jones and dug in his heels.

'I did it for Bob Geldof', wrote Townshend in *Who I Am*. 'But, at one point, when Bob sensed I might refuse to appear, he took the gloves off. "If The Who appear, we know we will get an additional million pounds of revenue", he said forcefully. "Every pound we make will save a life. Do the fucking maths. And do the fucking show."'

The Who reconvened a few days ahead of Live Aid for two days of rehearsals. Jones recalled: 'We met up, ate a bacon sandwich, talked all day, then ran through two numbers and went home.'

The Who took to the stage just before 8:00 pm. They kicked off with 'My Generation' – a song that was already 20 years old. Only 30 seconds in, a massive technical failure led to a breakdown in the TV transmission. Ironically, Roger Daltrey was just about to sing, 'why don't you all fade away?'

'They were unaware of this technical hitch, but even still, they seemed unsure of themselves and under-rehearsed', wrote Paul Rees in *The Ox:*

> There was also something forced and joyless about their performance. Entwistle looked subdued and dressed it, too, in a tan leather jacket and jeans. Townshend, pale, rail-thin and balding, dutifully windmill-armed his guitar and scissor-kicked, but like an actor now, playing a role. Meanwhile, Daltrey, bare-chested and stone-faced, seemed blank and disengaged from everything and everyone around him, but most especially from Jones, who played just as ably as he always had, but not to lift [the band's performance] from being above perfunctory.

Power was restored towards the end of the band's second song, 'Pinball Wizard'. A meaty 'Love Reign O'er Me' followed. Daltrey sings this truly classic song with every ounce of energy in his body. Listen also to John Entwistle's astounding bass playing.

They finish with 'Won't Get Fooled Again' as the sun sets on Wembley Stadium. They are just warming up, but three minutes in, Daltrey comes in too soon with the 'I move myself and my family aside' vocal refrain. There are a few moments of confusion as the band busk through the chord changes and ride out the cock-up.

Brian May: 'I watched The Who from the side of the stage and it was obvious they weren't getting on very well with each other. Sparks were flying – it was actually quite exciting.'

Pete Townsend: 'I wandered around a little, feeling out of place. Backstage, there was a great sense of community. I talked to Bono, who was never afraid of waxing lyrical at such times. We all felt proud to be there. As for our performance, The Who were out of practice and should probably have left it to Queen and George Michael, who stole the show.'

The Who would reunite in 1989. John Entwistle died in 2002. Against all odds, and 60 years on, Daltrey and Townshend continue to record and tour together.

Philadelphia: 20:21 BST/15:21 EDT – Santana With Pat Metheny

Introduced by Bill Graham
'Brotherhood' (Santana/Sancious/Thompson)
'Primera Invasion' (Santana /Lear/Margen/Pasqua)
'Open Invitation' (Santana/Lambert/Potter/Walker/Margen)
'Right Now' (Santana/Ligertwood)

There is no mention of Live Aid in Carlos Santana's autobiography and his band's performance is missing from the DVD and from both the official YouTube channel and downloads. This is odd because Santana's tight set was one of the best of the day.

Formed in 1966, Santana's booking at the Woodstock festival, their appearance in the hugely influential documentary (March 1970) and the end-to-end-wonderful album *Abraxas* (September 1970) increased their profile. *Abraxas* and its follow-up were number-one albums in the US. The singles 'Evil Ways', 'Black Magic Woman', 'Oye Cómo Va', 'Everybody's Everything', 'Winning' and 'Hold On' were top 20 singles in the US, as was their cover of The Zombies' 'She's Not There' in the UK.

Opting to ignore any familiar material, the band start with a new song from their latest album *Beyond Appearances.* The pedigree of these musicians, with their unique Mex-jazz hybrid, is clear. 'Brotherhood' fizzes along and segues straight into 'Primera Invasion' from 1981's *Zebop!,* with the triple-attack percussionists going nuts.

'Open Invitation' from *Inner Secrets* (1978) introduces vocalist Greg Walker. Walker adds his powerful soul voice whilst two brilliant guitar solos shamelessly quote Jimi Hendrix. This might be the outstanding performance of the Philly leg of Live Aid. It cooks.

Guest guitarist Pat Metheny joins the band for the close with a sparkling six-minute song, 'Right Now' from *Beyond Appearances.* The whole set can be found on YouTube at the time of writing. Forget 'Smooth'. This is the real deal.

London: 20:44 BST/15:44 EDT – Stavanger For Africa

'From All Of Us' (Røise)

David Hepworth introduces what claims to be the Norwegian equivalent of Band Aid, Forente Artister, or United Artists, with their song 'Sammen For Livet (Together For Life)', but is, in fact, 'From All Of Us' by Stavanger for Africa, a group of Norwegian artists from the Stavanger region in the south-west corner of Norway.

Written by Per Røise, who sings with his daughters Marianne and Elisabeth, the other artists are Per Inge Torkelsen, Steinar Lyse, Eli Furubotn, Mia Gundersen, Rita Eriksen, Sissel Riis, Lina Holt, Jon Dagsland, Sigvart Dagsland and Magne Høyland.

It's for a good cause.

London: 20:50 BST/15:50 EDT – Elton John With Kiki Dee And Wham!

Introduced by Billy Connolly
'I'm Still Standing' (John/Taupin) – Official releases: digital download
'Bennie And The Jets' (John/Taupin) – Official releases: digital download/DVD/YouTube
'Rocket Man' (John/Taupin) – Official releases: digital download/DVD/YouTube
'Don't Go Breaking My Heart' (John/Taupin) – Official releases: digital download/DVD/YouTube
'Don't Let The Sun Go Down On Me' (John/Taupin) – Official releases: digital download/DVD/YouTube
'Can I Get A Witness' (Holland/Dozier/Holland) – Official releases: digital download

Elton John launches George Michael's solo career.

It's easy to forget that Our Reg was seriously out of fashion as the seventies flipped to the eighties. After ten massive albums between 1970 (the year of 'Your Song') and 1978, a split with lyricist Bernie Taupin and a disastrous foray into disco on *Victim Of Love,* John would suffer a career dip that might have finished lesser artists. 1983's *Too Low For Zero* and the massive 'I'm Still Standing' marked a return to form.

The set was carefully rehearsed at Elstree Studios with John's long-time side man Davey Johnstone on guitar and new bassist David Paton. Paton wrote in his memoirs:

> July 12 was a sleepless night. The house was full of excitement. As we watched it on TV at home, I found it hard to believe I'd be there on stage with Elton that evening. A limousine arrived late afternoon and took Mary and me to London, where we met up with the band and were driven to Wembley by private bus. There were 13 of us and we were joined by Billy Connolly, Pamela Stephenson, Kiki Dee… When we arrived, we were taken to our dressing room area and then invited to a VIP area to watch David Bowie perform his set. I can't really put into words the excitement and atmosphere in the stadium; it really was an amazing event. If you're a musician and you've been to a big event like this, you'll know that when you watch other performers, you just get eager to get up there and play. I was like that. I was going on stage with Elton John and I just couldn't wait to play my bass in front of this massive crowd. The dressing room area was set out within a huge circle with tables, chairs and parasols in the centre. I saw Paul and Linda McCartney arrive to a huge flurry of activity. Many bands and solo artists were sitting at the tables and chatting. It was a great thing to see your heroes all mixing, laughing, chatting and relaxing in the sun. I'd be lying if I said I wasn't nervous.

Almost nine hours after 'Rocking All Over The World', Elton John opened his set with the effervescent 'I'm Still Standing' after an introduction from Billy Connolly, who claimed that 'this concert is being shown on 95% of the televisions on Earth'.

Elton is soberly dressed, by his standards, in a feathered Cossack hat and shiny jacket. There are horrendous sound problems, but, ever the pro, even after six months off the road, he sounds sharp and in good voice. The irony of singing 'I'm Still Standing', a song about facing adversity and overcoming it, is not lost on the viewer, as each line of vocal is marred by feedback and the band sound like a distant rumble punctuated by shrill horns.

The sound improves markedly for the evergreen 'Bennie And The Jets', which shines. Two minutes in, he casually leans on the piano while keeping in time, playing the song with one hand, engaging the audience and singing.

Thrillingly, the crowd sings along to the classic 'Rocket Man'. Elton hits all the high notes with flawless falsetto – voice problems in 1987 necessitated surgery and he never quite sounded the same again. Guitarist Davy Johnstone lathers delicious slide across everything. Perfect.

Kiki Dee steps forward for 'Don't Go Breaking My Heart', John's only number-one single at that point. Dee is sassy and soulful. The warmth between the pair is palpable.

Elton warmly introduces George Michael and Andrew Ridgely, the duo that make up Wham! Here was a showcase for George Michael, lightly bearded and wearing a leather jacket, white T-shirt and sunglasses. With Ridgeley joining Dee and the other backing singers, George stays centre stage for a heartfelt rendition of 'Don't Let The Sun Go Down On Me'.

Michael is slightly off-pitch in the first couple of verses, but he warms up as the chorus kicks in and pulls off a memorable, charismatic performance, which surprised many viewers, especially with the startlingly controlled riff on 'see me once and see the way I feel'. Elton beams like a proud parent. The last chorus is quite brilliant. Astonishingly, Michael had just turned 22.

For the moment, George Michael would concentrate on Wham! and their planned US stadium tour. But he was edging closer towards a solo career. 'Careless Whisper' was a number one in 1984 and 'A Different Corner' would repeat this chart position in spring 1986. Within a year of that, he would be a global superstar. Live Aid and this one song was the catalyst.

Elton John closed his set with one of his favourite soul songs – Marvin Gaye's 'Can I Get A Witness'. Again, sound problems mar the performance, but Elton is on peak form, especially in the breakdown section with his backing singers.

Everyone remembers Queen at Live Aid, and rightly so, but rewatch Elton John and marvel.

Philadelphia: 20:57 BST/15:57 EDT – Ashford And Simpson With Teddy Pendergrass

'Solid' (Ashford/Simpson)
'Reach Out and Touch (Somebody's Hand)' (Ashford/Simpson) – Official releases: digital download/DVD/YouTube

Philly overlaps with London for the husband-and-wife songwriting, production and recording duo Nickolas Ashford and Valerie Simpson. As staff writers with Motown, they worked with Marvin Gaye, Diana Ross, Gladys Knight and many others. From 1977 onwards, they achieved a series of gold albums. 'Solid' was an international hit in 1984 and somewhat shakily opened their short, two-song set.

It's all very 1980s, with shoulder pads, teeth, flowing satin shirts and ozone-depleting hair products. 'Solid' is marred by sound problems and is absent from all official releases.

Nick Simpson introduces former Blue Notes singer Teddy Pendergrass for a scintillating version of the Ashford and Simpson penned 'Reach Out And Touch (Somebody's Hand)', written for Diana Ross. Live Aid was Pendergrass' first public performance after a serious car accident in 1982, which left him in a wheelchair. He cannot hold back a tear as the band vamps behind him. When he starts to sing, the crowd go nuts and the viewer gets goosebumps. It's a special moment.

Pendergrass died in 2010, and Ashford in 2011.

Studio: 21:19 BST/16:19 EDT – Kool And The Gang

'Stand Up And Sing' (Bell/Bell/Bonnefond/Brown/Smith/Taylor/Williams)
'Cherish' (Bell/Bell/Bonnefond/Brown/Smith/Taylor/Williams)

The American soul-funk band Kool and the Gang had a string of hits between 1979 and 1985. Their most recent, the romantic ballad 'Cherish', was a huge song all over the world.

James 'JT' Taylor, Dennis 'Dee Tee' Thomas and Robert 'Kool' Bell had sung on 'Do They Know It's Christmas?' – the only American act to take part – so their inclusion in the Live Aid line-up was a logical development.

Although it was widely reported that the band appeared on stage in Philadelphia, their contribution was pre-recorded.

Philadelphia: 21:27 BST/16:27 EDT – Madonna

Introduced by Bill Graham
'Holiday' (Hudson/Stevens-Crowder) – Official releases: digital download/DVD/YouTube
'Into The Groove' (Ciccone/Bray) – Official releases: digital download/DVD/YouTube
'Love Makes The World Go Round' (Ciccone/Leonard)

Madonna's long string of hit singles began with the chirpy 'Holiday' in September 1983. She opens her set with this song, looking young and confident. Her vigorous dance routine results in very pitchy vocals, but the band are super-tight, with producer Pat Leonard on keyboards. The crowd lap it up.

Rather cheekily, her second song was the yet-to-be-released 'Into The Groove', which was featured in the film *Desperately Seeking Susan* but was not yet commercially available. Made available two days after Live Aid, the exposure pushed the song to the top of the charts in many countries around the world, including the UK, where it was the first of her 13 number ones. Her performance is raw and energetic.

Rather than singing one of her huge hits – 'Borderline', 'Like A Virgin', 'Material Girl', 'Crazy For You' or 'Angel' – her closing number is the interminable 'Love Makes The World Go Round' in its only live performance. It would be released over a year later on *True Blue* and then promptly forgotten. The Thompson Twins and Nile Rodgers provide backing tambourines on a forced, pitchy and slack performance, which suffers from touches of microphone feedback and improves immeasurably when she stops singing in the middle eight. A misstep.

London: 21:48 BST/16:48 EDT – Freddie Mercury And Brian May

Introduced by John Hurt
'Is This The World We Created...?' (Mercury/May) – Official releases: digital download/DVD/YouTube

For the first part of the Wembley finale, Queen's Freddie Mercury and Brian May return to sing the heartfelt, acoustic and wholly appropriate 'Is This The World We Created...?' from their album *The Works*. Mercury's vocal prowess is a stunning masterclass in control and power. At one point, on the line, 'You know that every day a helpless child is born/Who needs some loving care inside a happy home', he almost breaks down in tears. His final note is simply awesome. Mercury nods to himself at a job well done. It's a beautiful performance.

London: 21:51 BST/16:51 EDT – Paul McCartney

'Let It Be' (Lennon/McCartney) – Official releases: download/DVD/YouTube

This was Paul McCartney's first live performance since 29 December 1979. A failed microphone can hardly have helped his nerves, as unfortunately for him – and for us watching on the day – his vocals were inaudible for the first two minutes. In what seems like an impromptu decision, Bob Geldof, David Bowie, Alison Moyet and Pete Townshend returned to the stage to sing with him in the final choruses, messing up their cue and singing some incorrect lines. But as a moment, it was glorious. McCartney re-recorded his vocals the following day so that DVD and online viewers can enjoy one of the greatest musicians doing what he does best.

London: 21:57 BST/16:57 EDT – Band Aid

'Do They Know It's Christmas?' (Geldof/Ure) – Official releases: digital download/DVD/YouTube

The 29th act and last song at Wembley was a Christmas tune in the middle of July. Bob Geldof recalled:

> Everyone came on for the finale. There was a tremendous feeling of oneness on that stage. There had been no rivalry, no bitching and no displays of temperament all day. Now everyone was singing. They had their arms around each other. Elton was crying; everyone was crying. Not the easy tears of showbiz but genuine emotion. Down in the crowd, the punters were crying. Even some of the photographers crowding around the stage were crying. The performance was still a shambles, but perhaps the audience were prepared for that.

Francis Rossi:

> At the end of a very long and crazy day, we were all rounded up and taken to the back of the stage, ready to try and find a place for ourselves onstage to sing the final song, 'Do They Know It's Christmas?', which I really didn't want to do. I was sitting with David Bowie and Steve Van Zandt when they came to round us up. Then, just as we stood up, all the lights went out and the table we were sitting at collapsed. We were all laughing hysterically, bumping into each other trying to make our way to the stage and only just getting there in time. As I got onto the side of the stage, I saw Rick [Parfitt]. He seemed to be having the time of his life.

'I think you know the next song', Geldof declares on stage. 'It might be a bit of a cock-up, but if you're gonna cock it up, then ya may as well do it with two billion people watching yis.'

Gary Kemp:

> The show's finale, the big 'Feed The World' sing-along, and the chance to hang out onstage 'equally' with the greats of pop. Even there, the hustle and bustle of standing next to and with the right person is apparent, McCartney and Geldof being the magnets, the messianic glimmer twins of the evening. Here's George Michael, not hiding his light at all, setting himself up centre stage by the Irish one. Then there's Bono, squeezing in. Freddie's up close and personal, too, his band having created what will now become a Queen renaissance. And as for us? Well, we're a little squeezed out right now, trapped behind Macca's piano and a few session players stage right. We just didn't get to the front in time. Once the race was on, if you were slow but still wanted the middle, you ran the risk of ending up looking like a

fairground head, bobbing up and down at the back. We wanted the front of the stage, but unfortunately, by the time we arrived, that meant being out of shot and out of any reflected glory. How fast those big stars are! But maybe, just maybe, it wasn't lack of speed we suffered from but something else: not feeling worthy enough. Subconsciously, we held back – eternal fans who knew their place.

David Bowie sings the opening lines as dozens of performers anxiously read the lyrics from sheets. Paul McCartney leaps with joy; the crowd come in too soon with the 'Let them know it's Christmas time' refrain; Freddie Mercury looks like he doesn't have a clue what's going on and Bono makes an arse of himself. But as a memorable – no, let's say historic – moment, this is an 'I was there' or 'I was watching' once-in-a-lifetime slice of the 1980s. The crowd were going absolutely nuts.

The song's co-writer, Midge Ure, is hiding at the back of the stage. 'It was more important that the cameras focused on Bob, George Michael, Bono, Macca and Bowie,' he wrote, 'that was the hierarchy of the whole show. The shot that people were going to see all around the world was this mass gathering, the best musicians that Britain had to offer all on stage, all singing the same song. I was there. That is good enough for me. After all, they were singing my song.' Mid-song, Ure is pulled to the front of the stage to share a microphone with Bob Geldof. It's an emotional moment and much deserved.

And, one minute over time, that was it. At Wembley Stadium, at least.

Midge Ure: 'I got stuck driving through the streets of Wembley with all the audience squished up around the car, walking home or back to the tube. People were throwing open their doors and having parties. It was like Hogmanay in Glasgow. People were inviting complete strangers off the street into their homes. This is London; that just doesn't happen. But it happened that night.'

Mark Ellen was heading into central London:

From my cab, the whole of London looked deserted. From Wembley to Piccadilly Circus, there was barely a soul to be seen. Windows were wide open in the blistering heat and I kept catching the sound of the broadcast. Live Aid was blaring from radios in passing cars and parks and from TVs in pubs, flats and gardens. Sometimes, I heard everyone singing the same song all down the street. The air had the warm scent of smoke and scorched steak. It was extraordinary: those love affairs we'd all had with scratchy old records made by radicals that our parents hated and the newspapers mocked or ignored had somehow blossomed into a mass mainstream movement that could motivate millions of people all over the world to feel the same way in the same moment. Pop music had made this happen, pop music and the mechanics of the new media.

'As I went home that night,' writes Dylan Jones, 'having spent all day in the Wembley sun, huddled on the Tube, along with thousands of others who had sung along to the finale of 'Do They Know It's Christmas?' in the hot summer air, I felt as though pop had somehow entered another dimension, pushed itself through a vortex.'

Bob Geldof:

> We tried to find a car to take us back to London, but they had all gone. We hitched a lift from some people we met in the car park. It took us hours to get back to Chelsea, where I wanted to wash and change before going to Legends, the Bond Street nightclub, which had set up a large screen downstairs for us to watch the last third of the concert coming in from America. London was packed that night as we crawled through the summer night's traffic jam. People walked over to the car and hugged me. Some cried, 'Oh Bob, oh Bob', not sneering, not uncontrollable, just something shared and understood. 'I know' was all I could say. I did know. I wasn't sure what had happened in England or everywhere else, but I knew'. Somehow, something had gone right. Cynicism, greed and selfishness had been eliminated for a moment. It felt good. A lot of people had rediscovered something in themselves. This does sound pompous. Too bad.

The BBC moved their live broadcast to Legends nightclub on Old Burlington Street in central London, memorably described by the increasingly baggy-eyed co-presenter Andy Kershaw as 'one of those discreet and expensive basement nightclubs in Mayfair, the kind in which, on regular evenings, middle-aged aristocrats charm girls a third of their age – called Tamara – when they are not swapping stories about their part in getting 'Lucky' Lucan out of the country.'

Kershaw was joined by Mark Ellen and Mike Smith, who, at that time, was co-hosting the *Late, Late Breakfast Show.* In Philadelphia, meanwhile, the concert continued.

Philadelphia: 22:02 BST/17:02 EDT – Tom Petty And The Heartbreakers

Introduced by Bill Graham
'American Girl' (Petty) – Official releases: digital download/DVD/YouTube
'The Waiting' (Petty) – Official releases: YouTube
'Rebels' (Petty) – Official releases: YouTube
'Refugee' (Petty/Campbell) – Official releases: digital download/DVD/YouTube

By 1985, Tom Petty and the Heartbreakers had scored a hatful of minor hit singles in the US. Better still, their albums *Damn The Torpedoes, Hard Promises, Long After Dark* and *Southern Accents* (1979-1985) had each lodged in the top ten as the band built a reputation as a powerful, rocking and sometimes quirky concert band. Petty's sideburns might be questionable, but their skills as a live act – they were mid-way through a long American tour and as tight as Stan Campbell's snare – are displayed immediately with their opening 'American Girl', a truly timeless track which kicked off their first album and which the band decided to play just minutes before taking to the stage. Mike Campbell's chiming guitars hide a dynamic arrangement which blasts across JFK Stadium. Oh yeah, all right.

The Dylan-esque and hugely ironic 'The Waiting' was the lead single from The Heartbreakers' 1981 album *Hard Promises.* Petty chugs through the first two minutes on his own, and as the band kick in after the bridge, the place lifts off. Perfection. The hugely confident rallying cry of 'Rebels', the band's most recent single, confirms that this is a mighty live band and they take it home with 'Refugee', one of their biggest hits from spring 1980. They play like they're in a bar with 200 people, not at a huge outdoor gig being broadcast worldwide: the energy is almost tangible. Tight, loud, majestic and brilliant.

Petty's first solo album *Full Moon Fever* (April 1989) and his tenth album with the Heartbreakers, *Into The Great Wide Open* (July 1991), together with those killer live shows, finally brought him global success.

Petty died, aged 66, in 2017.

Philadelphia: 22:30 BST/17:30 EDT – Kenny Loggins

Introduced by Chevy Chase
'Footloose' (Loggins/Pitchford) – Official releases: digital download/DVD/YouTube

Like 'Money For Nothing', 'Uptown Girl, 'Let's Dance' and 'Dancing In The Dark' – songs which don't represent the best of four major performers – there was much more to Kenny Loggins than 'Footloose', a beard, great teeth, ridiculous suit and sculpted haircut.

Loggins made his name both as a songwriter and with the duo Loggins and Messina. Six hit albums between 1972 and 1976 led to a solo career that placed five top 20 singles in the US by the time he hit pay dirt with the irredeemably cheesy 'Footloose', the theme from the 1984 film and a US chart-topper for Loggins, which also hit number six in the UK.

The audience love it.

'Danger Zone' from the *Top Gun* soundtrack would give Loggins another huge hit in 1986. He's still on the road and singing like a bird.

Following this performance, the BBC broadcast showed 'Love Somebody' from Rick Springfield's set earlier in the day.

Philadelphia: 22:39 BST/17:39 EDT – The Cars

Introduced by Bette Midler
'You Might Think' (Ocasek) – Official releases: YouTube
'Drive' (Ocasek) – Official releases: YouTube
'Just What I Needed' (Ocasek) – Official releases: digital download/DVD/YouTube
'Heartbeat City' (Ocasek) – Official releases: digital download/DVD/YouTube

The four-piece band The Cars from Boston released five albums by 1985. They were top ten artists in the US but were lesser-well known outside their home country, despite their appealing mix of spiky, quirky guitar-based new wave (viz 'My Best Friend's Girl' from 1978) and the swirling balladry of their best-known song, 1984's 'Drive'.

They open with one of their best-known songs, 'You Might Think', archly sung by Rik Ocasek. It is appealing and tight, in and out in three minutes. In an age when MTV ruled – the promo for 'You Might Think' was Video of the Year at the first MTV Video Awards in 1984 – the band proved, effortlessly, that they could cut in on the live stage. The backing vocals are flawless.

Mid-way through this performance, a certain P. Collins landed at Philadelphia airport.

Bassist Benjamin Orr steps forward for a flawless rendition of the timeless 'Drive'. It's a sober moment. The refrain of 'we can't go on/thinking nothing's wrong' seemed appropriate for Live Aid's underlying cause.

Orr stays the focus of the bright, sardonic power pop of 'Just What I Needed' from 1978, which lightens the mood despite the crushing derision of its lyrics. They close with the title track of their current album *Heartbeat City*. This is perhaps too mid-tempo for such a large event, but it proves, if needed, that The Cars were a killer band.

Bassist Benjamin Orr died in 2000; guitarist and songwriter Ocasek died in 2019.

Following this performance, the BBC broadcast 'Can't Fight This Feeling' from REO Speedwagon's set earlier in the day.

Philadelphia: 23:06 BST/18:06 EDT – Neil Young

Introduced by Joe Piscopo
'Sugar Mountain' (Young)
'The Needle And The Damage Done' (Young) – Official releases: digital download/DVD/YouTube
'Helpless' (Young) – Official releases: YouTube
'Nothing Is Perfect (In God's Perfect Plan)' (Young) – Official releases: digital download/DVD/YouTube
'Powderfinger' (Young) – Official releases: YouTube

Neil Young has always followed his own path. Even in group situations, such as Buffalo Springfield and CSN&Y, he was always the outsider. It's also entirely predictable that he would choose to play an unreleased song at Live Aid. Before that, he stands alone with his acoustic guitar and harmonica for the oldie 'Sugar Mountain', which opened his 1979 live album *Rust Never Sleeps* but dates back to 1965.

Typically, for an acoustic performance at Philadelphia, the sound takes a while to balance, but once it's set, his voice echoes across JFK and the crowd listen intently and sing lustily in the chorus. The minimalistic, hard-hitting 'The Needle And The Damage Done' is thrilling, visceral and astounding in its execution. The powerful 'Helpless' expresses the pain of loss. His band join in mid-way through, adding a country tint to a phenomenal performance. If there was ever a time for Crosby, Stills & Nash to come on stage, then this was it.

Just why Young thought it was a good idea to play the unheard 'Nothing Is Perfect (In God's Perfect Plan)' can only be answered by the man himself. It's something of a country dirge with trilling fiddles. In context, it's a nice song, but here, the words 'sore' and 'thumb' come to mind. 'Nothing Is Perfect (In God's Perfect Plan)' would not be released until 2011.

Finally, Young's vintage Les Paul, Old Black, gets an airing. Here, the paranoid, angst-ridden 'Powderfinger' gets a sprightly tempo and a dusting of country-style licks from fiddles and steel guitar. Young's guitar playing is delicious.

> Shelter me from the powder and the finger
> Cover me with the thought that pulled the trigger
> Just think of me as one you never figured

Yes, Neil Young has always followed his own path.

Following this performance, the BBC broadcast showed excerpts from 'Teach Your Children' and 'Suite: Judy Blue Eyes' from Crosby, Stills & Nash's set earlier in the day.

Philadelphia: 23:42 BST/18:42 EDT – The Power Station

Introduced by Don Johnson
'Murderess' (Palmer/Taylor/Taylor) – Official releases: YouTube
'Get It On' (Bolan) – Official releases: YouTube

The original idea for The Power Station was quite interesting: team up idiosyncratic vocalist Robert Palmer with two members of Duran Duran and the drummer from Chic, light the blue touch paper and retire to a safe distance.

Their self-titled debut album, released in March 1985, resulted in the hits 'Some Like It Hot' and a cover of T. Rex's 'Get It On'. However, Palmer did not want to perform live with the band despite a 37-date North American tour being booked to begin at the end of June. He was replaced with Michael Des Barres, who, for all of his skills as a frontman, is no Robert Palmer.

The Live Aid performance took place after the first eight dates of the band's tour. It all seems very forced. The subtleties of the album versions are rolled flat by Des Barre's 'look at me' approach. Tony Thompson, though, is superb.

Following this performance, the BBC broadcast 'Roll With The Changes' by REO Speedwagon and 'Human Touch' by Rick Springfield from their sets earlier in the day.

Philadelphia: 00:21 BST/19:21 EDT – Thompson Twins

Introduced by Bette Midler
'Hold Me Now' (Bailey/Currie/Leeway)
'Revolution' (Lennon/McCartney) – Official releases: digital download/DVD/YouTube

The Thompson Twins enjoyed a string of hits in 1983 and 1984, including an impressive top three placing for 'Hold Me Now' in the US in spring 1984. By 1985, their biggest hits were behind them. Bette Midler perhaps overstates them in her on-stage introduction as 'not identical but unsurpassable'.

Tom Bailey's singing is a touch pitchy on the seven-minute 'Hold Me Now', but the instrumental arrangement is exciting. Nile Rodgers sits in on guitar.

Less impressive is the cover of The Beatles' 'Revolution'. It's an eye-wateringly bad performance, well-intended but clearly under-rehearsed. The presence of Madonna, who bops about and taps a tambourine, adds nothing. Guest guitarist Steve Stevens looks and sounds utterly ridiculous.

They do win the prize for the biggest haircuts, though.

Philadelphia: 00:38 BST/19:38 EDT – Eric Clapton

Introduced by Bill Graham
'White Room' (Bruce/Baker) – Official releases: digital download/DVD/YouTube
'She's Waiting' (Clapton/Robinson) – Official releases: digital download/DVD/YouTube
'Layla' (Clapton/Gordon) – Official releases: digital download/DVD/YouTube

Eric Clapton's star was on the rise again after several years of slack albums and lacklustre concert tours.

Phil Collins and Eric Clapton had become friendly over the previous few years. 'I first met him when I was in the studio in London with John Martyn [in 1979]', Collins wrote in his autobiography:

> Our introduction went like this: John has played with Eric and knows him well. One tiring day during the *Grace & Danger* sessions, he's looking for something to brighten up his day and thinks Eric can help. So, John calls and asks if the pair of us can come over to Eric's house in Ewhurst, not far from Old Croft. Eric must have said no – John is the kind of chap who has a tendency to overstay his welcome, and here, he's suggesting popping down to score with me, a complete stranger. So we meet in a pub in Guildford. Eric doesn't know me from a bar of soap, but I do remember sitting with a pint of Guinness opposite one of my heroes. Me, quaffing pints in the pub with the guy I'd idolised at the Marquee… Unfortunately, for a while thereafter, I fear that Eric assumes I'm just someone who hangs about with John when he's shopping for drugs. But by the end of '79, Eric and I are very close. By the time [*Duke*] was released on 28 March 1980, we've already started the tour. That particular day is the middle of three nights at London's Hammersmith Odeon, which is when Eric Clapton finally realises I'm more than a pool-playing drinking pal. He actually sees that I'm a fellow musician, a revelation about which I later hear he's a little surprised. Eric and I will come to play significant roles in each other's lives, personally and professionally, for years to come.

Five years later, Collins was invited to produce Clapton's ninth solo album *Behind The Sun*. This was a commercial success, placing Clapton back in the UK top ten for the first time since 1978. He toured extensively in 1984 and 1985 and was mid-way through the second leg of a long North American tour when he received a call from an old friend. Clapton wrote:

> In the early part of that summer, I got a phone call from Pete Townshend asking if I would play in a charity event being organised by Bob Geldof to raise money for the victims of famine in Ethiopia. It was to be called Live Aid and to consist of two concerts played simultaneously in London and Philadelphia on 13 July and broadcast live on TV across the world. As it

happened, we were to be in the middle of a North American tour on that date. We were booked to play Las Vegas the night before, with shows in Denver on either side, so there were some pretty big leaps involved. I told Roger to cancel the Las Vegas show and called Pete to say we'd do it. Thank God we were in good shape with the band playing really well because had we just started our tour, I might have had second thoughts otherwise. Landing in Philadelphia the day before the show, one couldn't help but get swept up in the atmosphere. The place was just buzzing. The moment we landed, you could feel music everywhere. We checked into the Four Seasons Hotel, every room of which was filled with musicians. It was Music City, and like most people, I was awake most of the night before the concert. I couldn't sleep with nerves. We were due to go onstage in the evening and I sat watching the performances of the other acts on TV for most of the day, which was probably a psychological mistake, as seeing all these great artists giving their best made me a hundred times more psyched up than I would have been for a regular gig.

Despite 22 years as a professional musician, Clapton, who had just turned 40, was untypically anxious. 'By the time we got out to the stadium,' he wrote, 'I was in such a state of nerves that I was literally tongue-tied. It was also boiling hot, and the whole band felt faint.'

He opened with a rock-steady version of the old Cream classic 'White Room'. 'Things got off to a shaky start. When I moved up to the microphone to sing the first line of 'White Room', I got a great big shock off it, further unnerving me, and meaning that I had to sing the rest of the show with my mouth not quite touching the mic, but still close enough to hear myself since the monitors weren't very good.' You can see Clapton blink, flinch and step back on the phrase 'by the station'. Nevertheless, Clapton's closing guitar solo is remarkable in its power and fluidity.

This was followed by 'She's Waiting', the opening song from *Behind The Sun*. The band are super-tight and even if this is a lesser-known Clapton track – he only played it on this tour – his commitment is 100% and his singing is very good indeed. Collins and fellow drummer Jamie Oldaker kick up a storm.

The memorable set closes with the crowd-pleasing 'Layla'. A teasing 30-second instrumental precedes that famous guitar riff. The audience, as they say, go wild. And rightly so. Here is a major artist kicking off his mid-career prime. Immediately elected to rock royalty, Clapton's *Unplugged* album, a few years after Live Aid, would become the best-selling live album of all time, selling 26 million copies worldwide.

Back in London, at the post-Wembley event at Legends, the effervescent Sadu Adu was interviewed by Mark Ellen for the BBC broadcast. She confessed to being worn out by the day's events. 'I'm beyond flagging', she said. 'It's been fairly nerve-wracking for everyone involved. It's such a massive thing, and it's a bit like school sports day. I think it's a great success.'

'What was it like when you actually went on stage?' Ellen asked. 'You've probably got used to these enormous venues, haven't you?'

'Every week we play in front of 80,000 people, yes', she replied with a massive smile. 'I'm always nervous when I go on stage, but I don't think I was more nervous today, really, because there was quite a lot of spirit. Not alcohol. A bit of that, maybe. It's been so big, so vast, that you can't comprehend it. Therefore, it feels quite small in a way. It was a thrill to do it. The most impressive thing was everyone's spirit, all pulling together.'

Philadelphia: 01:00 BST/20:00 EDT – Phil Collins

Introduced by Jack Nicholson and Bette Midler
'Against All Odds (Take A Look At Me Now)' (Collins) – Official releases: YouTube
'In The Air Tonight' (Collins) – Official releases: digital download/DVD/YouTube

Sharp-eyed viewers will already have noticed Phil Collins sitting behind his drum kit during Eric Clapton's set. Collins had met Clapton and been told which songs he'd be playing just 30 minutes beforehand.

The chirpy musician remained on stage to reprise his two songs from Wembley ('good evening Philadelphia, good evening London, good evening the world'). Despite his 5,700-mile journey between stages, Collins is in fine voice, strong and defined after six months on tour. He doesn't fluff the piano this time.

Philadelphia: 01:10 BST/20:10 EDT – Led Zeppelin

Billed on the day as 'Phil Collins, Robert Plant, Jimmy Page and John Paul Jones'
Listed in the official Live Aid book as 'Plant, Page and Jones'
Introduced by Phil Collins
'Rock And Roll' (Bonham/Jones/Page/Plant)
'Whole Lotta Love' (Bonham/Jones/Page/Plant/Dixon)
'Stairway To Heaven' (Page/Plant)

Oh dear.

Backstage in Philadelphia, having woodshedded the songs by listening to his Walkman on Concorde, Phil Collins met the three ex-members of Led Zeppelin in a tense dressing room. Collins told *Classic Rock* in 2017: 'I listened to 'Stairway To Heaven' on Concorde. I arrived and went to the caravans and Robert said: "Jimmy Page is belligerent." Page says: "We've been rehearsing!" And I said: "I saw your first gig in London; I know the stuff!" Jimmy looks at me. "So," he says, part drawl, part growl, "you know what we're playing?" I feel like I've failed a test. What I think Jimmy's actually saying is: "Do we really need this guy? Do we really need him to be playing with us?" I'm made to feel like the guy who's gate-crashed the party.'

At 8.10 pm, with dusk settling, Collins joined a very ragged, disjointed Led Zeppelin, who were definitely out of practice. 'Robert told me Phil Collins wanted to play with us', Page explained to *The Scotsman* in 2007. 'I told him that was all right if he knew the numbers. But at the end of the day, he didn't know anything. We played 'Whole Lotta Love' and he was just there bashing away cluelessly and grinning. I thought that was really a joke.'

Collins said in 2017:

> I had a word with [co-drummer] Tony Thompson. I've played as two drummers a lot and it can be a train wreck – and I say: 'Let's stay out of each other's way and play simple.' Thompson, rest his soul, had rehearsed for a week and I was about to steal his thunder – the famous drummer's arrived! – and he kind of did what he wanted to do. You can see me miming, playing the air. It was very uncomfortable, and if I could have left that stage, I would have left halfway through 'Stairway…', if not earlier. But imagine the coverage of that? Walking off during The Second Coming? Who the fuck does Collins think he is? Geldof really would have had something to swear about.

'Rock And Roll' is ragged but exciting. Plant struggles to hit the high notes. 'Any requests?' Plant asks as they kick into an abbreviated, loud and uneven version of 'Whole Lotta Love'. The inevitable 'Stairway To Heaven' seems to go on forever. Page's guitar drags and his solo is sloppy. Goodwill just about gets them through, but the last five minutes are painful.

This performance was not included in the massive ten-hour, four-DVD box set released in 2004. 'Because, of course, they were ashamed of it,' Collins writes, 'And I find that I am usually the one blamed for it. It couldn't possibly be the holy Led Zep who were at fault. It was that geezer who came over on Concorde who wasn't rehearsed. He was the culprit. That show-off.'

If they ever make a Led Zeppelin biopic, then it's unlikely to conclude with a recreation of their performance at Live Aid.

Philadelphia: 01:39 BST/20:39 EDT – Crosby, Stills, Nash & Young

'Only Love Can Break Your Heart' (Young)
'Daylight Again/Find The Cost Of Freedom' (Stills)

Crosby, Stills, Nash & Young had been an on-again, off-again collaboration between 1969 and 1976. They managed a single collective album in this period and toured in 1969, 1970 and 1974. Several attempts at further album sessions fell apart, and by 1985, they had not sung together for nine years.

At the time, Neil Young was performing with his latest band The International Harvesters ahead of his latest release, the mostly horrible *Old Ways*. Crosby, Stills & Nash were on tour as a trio, still promoting their most recent album *Daylight Again*. They were booked separately for Live Aid and it was Graham Nash who suggested an on-stage reunion.

Young finished his own set around 6.30 pm. CSN&Y hit the stage two hours later. In the interim, the four had gathered in Crosby's trailer, warming up with Young's 'Only Love Can Break Your Heart'.

'Together again, Crosby, Stills, Nash & Young…'

'How y'all doing?' said Nash, who had changed into a black MTV t-shirt and alarming leather trousers. 'Surprise!'

As with other acoustic acts at Philadelphia, there were significant sound problems: when a vocal-harmony group cannot hear each other, disharmony is inevitable. Nevertheless, they proceeded with a tentative 'Only Love Can Break Your Heart', followed by Stills and Young retuning their guitars for a robust 'Daylight Again' and a shaky snippet of 'Find The Cost Of Freedom'. Lasting six minutes and two-and-a-half songs, the performance was over before many knew it had begun. It was certainly an anti-climax. As Neil Young told writer Nick Kent ten years later: 'Damn, you'd have thought our performance on Live Aid would have been enough to finish off any wave of nostalgia, wouldn't you?'

The Live Aid reunion prompted a more formal CSN&Y regrouping for their second collective album *American Dream,* released in 1988. It's almost wholly awful. Later reunions in 1999-2000, 2002 and 2006 were more successful.

David Crosby died in 2023, aged 81.

Philadelphia: 01:46 BST/20:46 EDT – Duran Duran

Introduced by Chevy Chase
'A View To A Kill' (Le Bon/Taylor/Taylor/Taylor/Rhodes/Barry)
'Union Of The Snake' (Le Bon/Taylor/Taylor/Taylor/Rhodes) – Official releases: digital download/DVD/YouTube
'Save A Prayer' (Le Bon/Taylor/Taylor/Taylor/Rhodes) – Official releases: digital download/DVD/YouTube
'The Reflex' (Le Bon/Taylor/Taylor/Taylor/Rhodes) – Official releases: DVD/YouTube

If the ropy performances of Led Zeppelin and Crosby, Stills, Nash & Young hadn't forced you to bed in the 13th hour of Live Aid, then brace yourself for 'The Bum Note Heard Around The World'.

Although this was the last performance by the band's classic line-up, and their first anywhere in 13 months, Duran Duran were at the peak of their power and popularity in 1985. Their theme song for *A View To A Kill* was number one in America on the day of Live Aid and they were coming off an impressive run of eight consecutive top-ten hits in the UK since mid-1982.

They had taken time away from performing live and this would be their first show since April 1984. They open, naturally enough, with 'A View To A Kill'. It starts strongly – their rhythm section was always very accomplished – and the track builds into the chorus, in which singer Simon le Bon negotiates some tricky high notes. Le Bon's voice wobbles on the second chorus – 'to fatal sounds, of broken dreams' – and breaks completely on 'the fatal kiss is all we *need'*. Andy Taylor holds back a smirk. Wisely, 'A View To A Kill' is not included on the official DVD or YouTube channel.

An uncertain, guitar-driven, strangely pedestrian version of 'Union Of The Snake' is followed by six minutes of a slightly flat 'Save A Prayer'. Their final number, 'The Reflex', spotlights John Taylor's funky bass lines and has an actual guitar solo.

Drummer Roger Taylor and guitarist Andy Taylor would leave the band in 1986. Andy Taylor says, 'After the Live Aid set, there were no congratulatory hugs or smiles: it was as if we were foreign from each other. This would be the last time we played together in two decades (sic). Constant bickering and hostility had left the atmosphere acrid with tension. We were tired of the incendiary arguments, the dark depressions, the bitter resentments. We were tired of the 24-hour attention.'

Duran Duran continued, with reasonable success. A full reunion of the Live Aid line-up in 2001 led to a number of lucrative concert tours and the 2004 studio album *Astronaut.* Andy Taylor left once more in 2006 but guested on three songs on the band's 2023 release *Danse Macabre,* thus bringing the Live Aid line-up together once again.

London: 02:11 BST/21:11 EDT – Cliff Richard

'A World Of Difference' (Hewitt) – Official releases: digital download/DVD/ YouTube

> I'd been driving up the M1, at the wheel of a speedboat, of course, with popular mid-1960s Irish vocal trio The Bachelors across the back seat, delivering – as we rushed by the turn-off for Dunstable – their evergreen hit, 'I Believe'. In my rear-view mirror, their faces, contorted with sincerity, had begun to look menacing. Things, I could sense, were about to turn ugly. I awoke with my cheek on a deep, soft, red carpet. I had fallen asleep under a spiral staircase. Somewhere. All around me were smart heels, of shoes male and female, and the babble and easy laughter of a cocktail party. 'Come on, Andy. Wake up, old boy. Time to interview Cliff Richard. It was my friend, Trevor Dann, *Whistle Test* producer and, on this day of particular madness, a producer of Live Aid. The reality to which Trevor had brought me round was only slightly less grotesque than my motorway skippering of Con, Dec and the other one whose name no one could ever remember. As I got to my feet, there in front of me, sitting on a stool, nursing an acoustic guitar and looking repellently wholesome for a national monument to the mortician's art, was every mum's favourite Bachelor Boy. It had been a long day.
> Andy Kershaw, *No Off Switch* (2011)

'A young lad has just walked in off the street with a guitar,' joked Kershaw, live on air. 'And the name of this minstrel is Cliff Richard!'

Cliff had performed at a gospel concert in Birmingham earlier that evening. His small-hours performance on self-accompanied acoustic guitar is solid enough.

'I had written ['A World Of Difference'] on my first visit to the third world', composer Garth Hewitt said on BBC Radio 2's *Wired For Sound: The Cliff Richard Story*. 'In fact, I think I'd just been to Haiti. And seeing the impact of poverty and thinking of the world I'd come from and the world I'd just seen and so on. And that's exactly what it's about. It isn't so much making any comment. It's just observing the contrast, which we were all very conscious of on that day.'

Philadelphia: 02:20 BST/21:20 EDT – Patti LaBelle

Introduced by Bette Midler
'New Attitude' (Rice)
'Imagine' (Lennon) – Official releases: digital download/DVD/YouTube
'Forever Young' (Dylan) – Official releases: digital download/DVD/YouTube
'Stir It Up' (Faltermeyer/Forsey)
'Over The Rainbow' (Arlen/Harburg)/'Why Can't I Get It Over' – Official releases: YouTube

Two Philadelphia acts take prime-time slots over the next hour. Firstly, powerhouse soul singer Patti LaBelle, who had come to prominence in the early 1970s as one-third of the vocal group Labelle alongside Nona Hendryx and Sarah Dash. Their best-known song, 'Lady Marmalade', remains a classic disco-soul-funk crossover.

By 1985, LaBelle was promoting her seventh solo album following the inclusion of two songs on the soundtrack of *Beverley Hills Cop*. Her Live Aid set opens with one of these, 'New Attitude', a top 20 hit from earlier in 1985. She is immediately 'on' with an astounding blast of energy. Deep-soul, gospel-tinged covers of John Lennon ('Imagine') and Bob Dylan ('Forever Young') bring the mood down. Her singing is simply phenomenal.

LaBelle's microphone fails for 'Stir It Up', the second track from *Beverley Hills Cop*. A stagehand provides a replacement, but this doesn't work either (or the sound techs cannot find the right channel to fade up). The band stop the song very early, then vamp as Patti finally gets a microphone that works. It's one of the few technical trainwrecks in a long and complex pair of concerts.

LaBelle gets back on track with an astounding, emotional 'Over The Rainbow'. One could argue that she riffs and trills so far from the melody that the song is lost, but there's no doubt that we have 100% commitment here. This segues into a short extemporisation called 'Why Can't I Get It Over' to close her set.

LaBelle's biggest hit was 'On My Own', a duet with Michael McDonald released in 1986.

Following this performance, the BBC broadcast 'Paranoid' from Black Sabbath's set earlier in the day.

Philadelphia: 02:50 BST/21:50 EDT – Hall And Oates With Eddie Kendricks And David Ruffin

Dionne Warwick introduced by Bill Graham
Hall & Oates introduced by Dionne Warwick
'Out Of Touch' (Hall/Oates)
'Maneater' (Allen/Hall/Oates) – Official releases: digital download/DVD/YouTube
'Get Ready' (Robinson)/'Ain't Too Proud To Beg' (Whitefield/Holland)/'The Way You Do The Things You Do' (Robinson/Rogers)/'My Girl' (Robinson/White) – Official releases: digital download/DVD/YouTube

The Philadelphia concert starts to draw to a close. Local heroes Daryl Hall and John Oates and their band perform double duty here, firstly with their own set and then as the backing group for Mick Jagger.

Since 1977, Hall and Oates enjoyed a long string of hit singles in the US, including six *Billboard* number ones. They open with their most recent (and last, as it transpired), 'Out Of Touch', from December 1984. Hall, and his massive hair, seems particularly geed up. This is followed by the Motown groove of 'Maneater', their fifth US number-one and biggest chart placement in the UK.

Hall and Oates introduce Eddie Kendricks and David Ruffin, two former members of The Temptations, for a 12-minute, four-part medley. Kendricks and Ruffin appeared with Hall and Oates at the famous Apollo in New York a few weeks ahead of Live Aid and opened with four of The Temptations' best-known numbers. One must bow to Hall and Oates for donating over half of their set to The Temptations' music and an under-represented music genre.

The medley starts with the effervescent 'Get Ready' from 1966 and the dynamic 'Ain't Too Proud To Beg' from the same year. The band are super tight. The Temps' first chart hit, 'The Way You Do The Things You Do' (edited from the official Live Aid DVD, presumably because of feedback problems), is followed by a solid performance of the signature 'My Girl'.

MTV move to a commercial break. The BBC coverage discusses postage stamps and interviews impressionist Rory Bremner.

Philadelphia: 03:15 BST/22:15 EDT – Mick Jagger With Tina Turner

Introduced by Bette Midler
'Lonely At The Top' (Jagger/Richards)
'Just Another Night' (Jagger) – Official releases: digital download/DVD/YouTube
'Miss You' (Jagger/Richards) – Official releases: digital download/DVD/YouTube
'State Of Shock' (Jackson/Hansen) – Official releases: digital download/DVD/YouTube
'It's Only Rock 'N' Roll (But I Like It)' (Jagger/Richards) – Official releases: digital download/DVD/YouTube

With The Rolling Stones off the road and barely speaking, Mick Jagger performed his first-ever solo set at Live Aid. It was his first live appearance since the end of the Stones' *Tattoo You* shows in 1982.

Backed by Hall And Oates' band, it's frankly doubtful that anyone, anywhere, wanted to hear two songs from Jagger's album *She's The Boss*. Nevertheless, he does his trademark strut and patent yowl on the Jagger-Richards song 'Lonely At The Top'. One cannot deny the energy of a man who was two weeks short of his 43rd birthday. Jagger sings particularly well on the single 'Just Another Night', working hard to push a song that was his most recent hit, creeping to 12 in the US and 32 in the UK in February-March 1985.

The crowd-pleasing 'Miss You' ups the ante: here is why Jagger was, and still is, one of rock's great frontmen. Eddie Kendricks and David Ruffin return to the stage to add some silky backing vocals. Kudos, too, to bassist Tom 'T-Bone' Wolk and drummer Mickey Curry, who both power the track superbly.

This was a precursor to the introduction of Tina Turner, just a year into her remarkable comeback. Turner, with ex-husband Ike, supported The Rolling Stones in 1966 and 1969. 'I was making a surprise appearance that night to sing two songs with Mick,' she wrote in her memoirs, 'and before we went onstage, we spoke briefly about the tempo. Hall and Oates were playing backup for Mick … and I was concerned that they were playing a little slow. I need momentum. I can't dance to slow. I said, "Mick, I don't know if this is going to work if they can't pick it up." He told me not to worry, that he would take care of it.'

Tina matches Mick step-for-step and whoop-for-whoop as they sing 'State Of Shock' – a huge 1984 hit by The Jacksons, on which Jagger guested – before a smooth segue into the Stones' classic 'It's Only Rock 'N' Roll (But I Like It)'. It's big, brassy and lots of fun, even after Jagger strips off his t-shirt. There's an odd moment when both singers go off stage to change costumes mid-song, which dissipates some of the energy. Jagger returns in spandex pants and a yellow sports jacket, Turner in a tiny leather skirt. 'I was wearing a tight-fitting black leather top and skirt,' she wrote, 'and I could see a naughty idea forming.' Jagger rips it off. This performance remains, 40 years on, simply sensational if just a tad ridiculous.

The Rolling Stones returned in 1986 with the dismal *Dirty Work*, which almost finished them off. But a return to live performances in 1989 re-established them as the world's greatest rock 'n' roll band. Tina Turner enjoyed a string of hits through the 1980s and 1990s before retiring to Switzerland. She died there, aged 83, in May 2023.

Philadelphia: 03:39 BST/22:39 EDT – Bob Dylan, Keith Richards And Ronnie Wood

Jack Nicholson introduced by Bill Graham
Bob Dylan introduced by Jack Nicholson
'Ballad Of Hollis Brown' (Dylan)
'When The Ship Comes In' (Dylan)
'Blowin' In The Wind' (Dylan) – Official releases: digital download/DVD/YouTube

It was after 3.30 am in the UK when Jack Nicholson introduced Bob Dylan, who performed a short and shambolic set with Keith Richards and Ronnie Wood. Fifteen hours after the Royal Salute, this was a flatulent end to the Philly leg of Live Aid, not only crushingly disappointing for Dylan fans but also manna for his detractors, who no doubt were quick to claim that the 44-year-old Dylan was past his best. 'Though many of the reasons behind Dylan's disastrous appearance at Live Aid, in front of an estimated two billion viewers, were beyond his command,' writes Clinton Heylin, 'it was perceived at the time as evidence that he could not even sing his old songs with any conviction, let alone write and perform new songs of quality.'

Bob Dylan to the *LA Times* in November 1985: 'They screwed around with us. We didn't even have any monitors out there. When they threw in the grand finale, at the last moment, they took all the settings off and set the stage up for the 30 people who were standing behind the curtain. We couldn't even hear our own voices, and when you can't hear, you can't play; you don't have any timing. It's like proceeding on radar.'

Yes, Dylan can blame poor monitoring and rogue guitars for the ropey performance, but he alone must be held responsible for the very strange choice of songs. All were from 1962-1963. 'The Ballad Of Hollis Brown' recounts the story of a starving American farmer who kills himself and his family. 'When The Ship Comes In' is a rallying cry against impending Judgement Day. Only 'Blowin' In The Wind' seems to fit the mood.

The notoriously gnomic Dylan does not explain himself, or even mention the event, in his scattergun *Chronicles Vol. 1,* and neither does Keith Richard in his own autobiography, *Life.* Ronnie Wood, naturally, goes into detail in his entertaining memoirs, simply titled *Ronnie.* Wood writes:

> Towards the middle of 1985 and back in New York, Dylan rang me up to ask if I wanted to do a charity gig with him. I said sure because I was always happy to do anything with Bob, and not long after that, he showed up at my house on West 78th Street to talk about what songs we might do. I knew all of his songs but hadn't ever played any on a stage. He was showing me chords when I wondered, 'How about if I get Keith in here, too?' Dylan said, 'Yeah, okay', so I rang Keith and started to explain, 'I'm here with Bob

> Dylan', when Keith blurted out, 'Bob who? Fuck you.' I said, 'Dylan's invited me to play some charity gig and I'm inviting you along, too…

The trio rehearsed – bootleg tapes prove this – but neither Wood nor Richards seemed to realise that they were due on stage at Live Aid. Wood writes:

> A truck pulled up, driven by Bob's daughter, and Bob hopped in. 'You coming?' he asked, 'We're on in Philadelphia, man.' 'Philadelphia?' That was 90 miles away and would take us at least an hour and a half, not counting time to get out of Manhattan. Bob said, 'Follow us.' So Keith and I got into the limo and told the driver, 'Follow that truck'… The show closed with Bob Dylan, backed by Keith and me. On the stairs up to the stage, Bob turned to us and said, 'Let's do 'Blowin' In The Wind'. I said, 'What?'. He repeated, 'We'll do 'Blowin' In The Wind', and by then, it was too late to argue with him because we were onstage. I couldn't believe it because that was the only song of his we hadn't rehearsed. Right in the middle of the song, one of Bob's guitar strings broke. I saw it, thought fast and took off my guitar and handed it to him, leaving me there in front of all those people, playing air guitar. I reached behind and was handed the broken-down remains of an axe that I could busk with a slide on.

Warren Zanes wrote:

> Some would say that it was just what Live Aid deserved. For all of its noble intentions, Live Aid carried within it all the hubris and bloat of the mega-event. But in the midst of that unfocused performance, between songs, Dylan made a passing comment that, for most among the massive audience, drifted unnoticed into the night-time air: 'I'd like to say that I hope that some of the money that's raised for the people in Africa, maybe they can just take a little bit of it, maybe one or two million maybe, and use it to, say, pay the mortgages on some of the farms, what the farmers here owe to the banks.'

This was hardly appropriate. But to give him his due, Dylan would support the subsequent Farm Aid initiative.

'Dylan bravely struck a discordant note among the self-congratulatory back-patters,' suggests Clinton Heylin, 'by asking the billions watching to remember those in their own country struggling from economic events beyond their control. Overlooking the distinction between someone struggling and someone starving, Dylan's speech sparked Willie Nelson's attempt to organise a further event solely to benefit American farmers.'

Dylan recruited the tight-as-a-drum Tom Petty And The Heartbreakers as his support and backing band for the first Farm Aid, only seven weeks after Live Aid. Dylan toured the world in 1986 and 1987 with Petty, and this would establish him once again as a powerful, enervating live performer.

Bob Dylan is still Bob Dylan.

Philadelphia: 03:55 BST/22:55 EDT – USA For Africa

'We Are The World' (Jackson/Richie) – Official releases: digital download/DVD/YouTube

Lionel Richie, whose presence had been tightly protected, floats onstage like a shoulder-padded deity and leads the ensemble in a sing-along finale.

'We are gathered at the back of the curtain now, in a mad jumble', wrote Joan Baez. 'Dylan is nearing the last verse of 'Blowin' In The Wind' and I laugh out loud when I think of [stage manager] Ken Kragen saying, "When Bob's finishing up 'Blowin' In The Wind', Lionel will appear from behind the curtain and put his arm around Bob and say, '"Bob, we've got some of your friends here tonight"', and the curtain will open and there we'll all be!" Dylan will hate it. He can't stand anything going on behind his back.'

'When we finished our last song,' wrote Ron Wood, 'we turned around to find, to our surprise, the entire cast gathered behind us, breathing down our necks.'

Joan Baez: 'We are all laughing and hugging and waiting for the big moment. Dylan finishes his song. The curtains are opening. Dylan looks confused and tiny next to Lionel, with his smiling face and easy manner. The familiar chords begin and ... Lionel begins to sing and the audience is screaming. The stars have fanned out over the whole stage. I grab the mic with one hand and Chrissie [Hynde]'s hand tight with the other, and we give it all we have.'

Many of the day's performers returned to the stage to be joined by several guests, including Don Johnson, Cher and the sixties folk trio Peter, Paul And Mary.

Lines are sung by Lionel Richie, Harry Belafonte, Chrissie Hynde, Joan Baez, Sheena Easton, Dionne Warwick, Melissa Manchester, Kenny Loggins and Patti Labelle, who, as the last featured vocalist, hogs the microphone and wails indiscriminately. Bob Dylan stands centre stage, looking utterly lost. Eric Clapton adds some bluesy guitar licks.

'There we stand, singing our lungs out', writes Joan Baez. 'I am very happy. In fact, I could stay there all night. We can hear Patti and Dionne and Melissa and Lionel, and the rest is a great hodgepodge. Lionel is waving at us to shush and let the audience sing along. Everyone shushes except for Patti and Dionne. I listen to the exhilarated, sunburned, saturated audience and wonder what the day has meant to them and what it will continue to mean ... eventually, the song is over and all the stars are people and all the people are stars, and the day is over.'

'I didn't want 'We Are The World' as the last song,' wrote Bill Graham. 'I wanted 'Blowin' In The Wind'...'

The DVD uses the audio from the original single to cover up dead microphones. This gives us the voice of Kenny Rogers despite his absence from the concert.

The BBC broadcast closed down at 4:12 am. Over £2.5 million had been donated by UK viewers over the previous 16 hours.

'For around ten days, I learned what it was like to be truly famous', wrote Andy Kershaw. 'Not just well-known but in that bracket of public recognition alongside mainstream television personalities, pop idols, film stars and mass murderers. Everywhere I went, carrying out the most routine activities, I was conscious of people staring, openly pointing or asking for autographs. But within a fortnight, normality was restored. And, reassuringly, the bloke on the tube, or the girl in the pub, was again insisting I was John Noakes.'

'Live Aid changed the power of television,' wrote Mark Ellen, 'forged a bond between charity and celebrity and revitalised two decades of music, but it fell at its final hurdle. It seemed to have ushered in a return to rock 'n' roll altruism, but that was just a blip on the screen of a heart monitor and things slowly sank back to normal. Soon, it was just a warmly remembered, self-contained moment in a time of political selfishness. It wasn't the beginning of a new era. It was the slamming of the door on the old one.'

Epilogue

Both Wembley Stadium in London and JFK Stadium in Philadelphia have been demolished. We have lost Rick Parfitt, Alan Lancaster, Garry Roberts, Freddie Mercury, John Entwistle, David Bowie, three of the Four Tops (Levi Stubbs, Obie Benson and Lawrence Payton), Jam Master Jay, David Crosby, Carl Wilson, Nickolas Ashford, Teddy Pendergrass, Tom Petty, Ric Ocasek, Benjamin Orr, Eddie Kendrick, David Ruffin, Tom 'T-Bone' Wolk, Tina Turner and Harry Belafonte.

Of course, as well as raising the profile of the crisis in Ethiopia, many of the performers at Live Aid would see their stock rise instantly. Live Aid's most immediate impact was on the charts. The UK albums chart on 21 July 1985 saw improved placings for Dire Straits (at number two and 40), Paul Young (five), Phil Collins (six and 30), Madonna (ten), U2 (12, 16 and 32), Queen (*Greatest Hits* rose from number 72 to 17 three years after its release), Sade (21), Tina Turner (25), Alison Moyet (31), Howard Jones (44) and Ultravox (50). Indeed, only acts who had performed at Live Aid went up the charts that week. Likewise, the *Billboard* albums for 20 July saw 17 entries by Live Aid performers.

In 1986, Geldof received an honorary knighthood from Queen Elizabeth II for his efforts. He started a solo career after The Boomtown Rats' last gig in Dublin in May.

Meanwhile, the charity single dominated for the next few years. Notwithstanding the very worthwhile causes, punters had to contend with Tears For Fears' reworking of 'Everybody Wants To Rule The World' as the grammatically challenging 'Everybody Wants To Run The World' for Sport Relief. Two years later, Status Quo offered 'Running All Over The World'.

Multi-artist re-recordings of previous hits were worthy but generally one-time-listen affairs. Gerry Marsden re-did 'You'll Never Walk Alone' with a random selection of singers, actors and television personalities, billed as The Crowd, in aid of the Bradford City stadium fire. This was followed by 'Let It Be', credited to Ferry Aid to raise money for the Herald of Free Enterprise disaster at Zeebrugge. The appalling events at Hillsborough in 1989 led to 'Ferry Cross The Mersey' by a number of Liverpool artists. Little Steven Van Zandt drew some heavy hitters for the terrific 'Sun City' by Artists United Against Apartheid, which mixed dance and rap and a catchy chorus. And who can forget Cliff Richard and the Young Ones' toe-curling new version of 'Living Doll' for Comic Relief? Well, we can try.

Less artistically relevant was Pat Sharp and Mick Brown's trio of charity singles 'Let's All Chant' (1988) 'I Haven't Stopped Dancing Yet' (1989) and 'Use It Up And Wear It Out' (1990). Hale and Pace's 'The Stonk' (1991), despite its impressive rota of rock musicians and number one chart placing, is best forgotten.

A reworking of 'Do They Know It's Christmas?' in 1989, as Band Aid II, included such major stars as Big Fun, D Mob, The Pasadenas and

Technotronic. The song was recorded again in 2004 and 2014 and was a number-one on each occasion.

It was all for a good cause. You can spend an entertaining afternoon watching these on YouTube.

Bob Dylan's comments on stage at Philadelphia led indirectly to the first Farm Aid concert, organised by Willie Nelson and John Mellencamp to raise money for family farmers in the United States. This was held in Champaign, Illinois, on 22 September 1985. This has been a more-or-less annual event each year since then.

Many further 'Aid' concerts and tours followed. Self Aid in Dublin, 17 May 1986, highlighted enduring unemployment in Ireland. Performers at the event included U2, Van Morrison and The Pogues. The following month saw the Conspiracy of Hope tour: six concerts for Amnesty International with U2, Sting, Joan Baez, Lou Reed, Jackson Browne, The Neville Brothers and, at the final three concerts, a reunion of The Police.

A more political version of Live Aid took place at Wembley Stadium on 11 June 1988. The Nelson Mandela 70th Birthday Tribute marked the forthcoming 70th birthday of the still-imprisoned anti-apartheid revolutionary and included sets by Eurythmics, UB40, Simple Minds, Whitney Houston, Dire Straits and many others. For this, Midge Ure formed an 'all-star band', reprising an idea used at Princes' Trust concerts in 1982, 1986 and 1987.

A bizarre event called SOAP Aid, held at the rugby league stadium in St. Helens on 27 July 1988, mixed the cast of *Grange Hill* singing 'Just Say No' and *Coronation Street*'s Percy Sugden playing the ukulele, with sets from Marillion and Icicle Works. 'Soap Aid [was] a badly conceived follow up to Live Aid', Marillion's keyboardist Mark Kelly recalled. 'Various soap stars took it in turns to embarrass themselves on stage until, as the headliners, we trooped on to play. During 'Garden Party', a fight broke out which got so gallingly bad that [their singer] Fish asked us to stop playing while he attempted to pour oil on troubled (not to mention soapy) waters.'

The much more acceptable Human Rights Now! tour spanned six weeks in Autumn 1988, starting at Wembley Stadium. The shows featured Bruce Springsteen and the E Street Band, Sting, Peter Gabriel, Tracy Chapman and Youssou N'Dour, plus guest artists from each of the countries where concerts were held.

Less than seven years after Live Aid, many of the same performers paid homage to that event's most memorable performer at the Freddie Mercury Tribute Concert, which raised funds for the Mercury Phoenix Trust. Once again at Wembley Stadium, on 20 April 1992, the surviving members of Queen invited many musicians to play with them, including several who appeared at Live Aid: Roger Daltrey, Robert Plant, Paul Young, David Bowie, George Michael and Elton John.

A four-disc DVD set of most of the performances at Live Aid was released in 2004. Viewers who watched the whole concert on the day might feel a little short-changed, but the sound and picture quality are very good indeed. Around nine hours of audio was officially released as a digital download in 2018, as well as 87 videos on the official YouTube channel.

Looking back, if pop music was born on 27 January 1956 (the release of 'Heartbreak Hotel') and matured on 26 May 1967 (*Sgt Pepper's Lonely Hearts Club Band*), then it hit middle age on 13 July 1985. Pop music suddenly had principles: its early stars were middle-aged or dead and the likes of McCartney, Jagger and John were, or soon would be, establishment figures.

'Before Live Aid,' suggests Mark Ellen, 'certain people like Van Morrison and Rod Stewart or whatever were considered to be super antiquated. But when [the public] saw Live Aid, they saw a lot of bands that they hadn't heard of and they quite liked them. Also, people thought, "I'd forgotten about Queen, I'd forgotten about David Bowie and I saw them and they were wonderful, and actually, the stadium experience looks very pleasant. Like it might be a worthwhile venture to go to see people in places like that." So this was the beginning of the heritage industry.'

This is personified by the Sunday afternoon Legends slot each year at the immense (and televised) Glastonbury Festival. It's inconceivable that the likes of Kenny Rogers, Neil Diamond or Cat Stevens would have been booked at a show of this size without the rose-tinted view of musical acts that started with Live Aid. Those with a little more kudos – and actual Live Aid experience – would headline on the Saturday or Sunday night with career-defining performances: David Bowie (2000), Elton John (2023) and others.

Dylan Jones writes in *The Eighties: One Day, One Decade:*

> By the time of Live Aid, pop was exactly 30 years old, and in a way, the event was pop's apotheosis. After this, everything would eventually start to fragment as the power shifted from rock to dance, from white to black and from the cult of celebrity to the cult of the dance floor. Live Aid caused a quantum shift in the entertainment industry. The stadium became the de facto benchmark of success (if you couldn't fill a stadium three nights running, then you weren't properly successful). This was the point where pop diverged again, where mainstream rock acts went in one direction and underground dance music created an alternative culture that would soon rival rock in its omnipotence.

'The only drawback with Live Aid', notes Genesis' keyboard player Tony Banks in *Genesis: Chapter And Verse,* 'was that it was the point at which pop music became the establishment, a defining moment when suddenly it developed a conscience. Paradoxically, something died at the same time.'

Paul McCartney would again be wheeled out to close the 1986 Prince's Trust concert; the Let It Be Liverpool charity concert (1990); the Music For Monserrat fundraiser (1997); the Concert for New York City (2001); Live 8 (2005); the 39th Superbowl (2005); the Grammy Awards (in 2006, 2009, 2012 and 2015); Change Begins Within (2009); the London Olympics opening ceremony (2012); and the Queen's Diamond Jubilee (2012).

'After 13 July 1985, almost overnight, McCartney was suddenly a national treasure,' wrote Dylan Jones, 'a Queen Mother-type character, to be treated with care instead of caution. From here on in, McCartney became the default get, the grand finale to everything, from the Grammys to the Super Bowl. We almost expected him; to not have him somehow cast doubt over the proceedings. I mean, what kind of awards ceremony is this if Macca isn't here? Honestly!'

McCartney was knighted in 1997. Since then, a further four of Live Aid's participants have been knighted: Elton John (1998), Mick Jagger (2003), Brian May (2023) and, yes, Cliff Richard (1995). The horrendous Party at the Palace in 2002 was the event where 'classic' pop rolled over and died. Many of Live Aid's performers were dragged out: McCartney, of course, along with Bryan Adams, the surviving nub of Queen, half of Black Sabbath, Elton John, Brian Wilson, Eric Clapton and, naturally, Phil Collins. Oh, and Cliff Richard. The event was cringe-inducing, exemplified by Brian May posing with his guitar and bespoke trench coat blasting 'The National Anthem' high above Her Maj's London gaff. This is best forgotten.

An official sequel, Live 8, restored the balance. U2, Paul McCartney, Elton John, Bryan Adams, Madonna, Sting (reprising most of his Live Aid set), Bryan Ferry (this time with Roxy Music), The Who, George Michael and co-organisers Bob Geldof and Midge Ure all appeared at the London event, held in Hyde Park on 2 July 2005. Twin events around the world added Neil Young and Brian Wilson in Barrie and Berlin.

Even after 40 years, Live Aid still continues to make cultural waves. October 2018 saw a note-for-note, step-for-step recreation of Queen's performance in the film *Bohemian Rhapsody.* That same year, the Sky Arts TV series *Urban Myths* reimagined the scenes backstage at Live Aid in a brilliant parody, in which Elton John has a hissy fit about Noel Edmonds' helicopter landing on his begonias, Freddie Mercury has a crush on Bono ('Boner?') and Midge Ure accuses Bob Geldof of no longer being able to 'land on the beat'. It's marvellous.

In spring 2024, Live Aid was turned into a stage musical. *Just For One Day* featured songs played that day by acts including Queen, U2, Elton John, Paul McCartney and Sting. 'This isn't a tribute thing', Bob Geldof told the BBC. 'I wouldn't have anything to do with that. So, there isn't a person dressed up as Freddie wearing a crap moustache. The songs drive the drama along. The story is based on actual testimony from the day. It's real people telling their story throughout this. So it's complex theatre.' The musical, by John O'Farrell and Luke Sheppard, was made with the full permission of the Band Aid Trust, which received 10% of ticket sales. Geldof himself was played by actor Craige Els. 'Let me be completely blunt', Geldof said. 'It's bad enough being Bob Geldof. It's slightly worse seeing someone else pretending to be you. The one upside for me is that stage Bob has got an amazing voice. Therefore, people will think I actually sing as good as that.'

For those of us who were around in 1985, Live Aid was one of those days that linger long in the memory for all the right reasons. An estimated 1.9 billion people across 150 countries probably agree.

Bibliography

Baez, J., *And A Voice To Sing With: A Memoir* (Simon & Schuster, New York, 2009)
Bego, M., *Sade* (Columbus Books, London, 1986)
--- *Tina Turner: Break Every Rule* (Rowman & Littlefield, Lanham, 2005)
Blake, M., *Is This The Real Life?* (Da Capo Press, Philadelphia, 2011)
Boy George With Bright, S., *Take It Like A Man* (Harpercollins, London, 1995)
Clapton, E., *Eric Clapton: The Autobiography* (Cornerstone, London, 2010)
Collins, P., *Not Dead Yet: The Autobiography* (Crown Publishing Group, New York, 2016)
Costello, E., *Unfaithful Music And Disappearing Ink* (Blue Rider Press, New York, 2015)
Crosby, D. And Gottlieb, C., *Long Time Gone: The Autobiography Of David Crosby* (Dell, New York, 1990)
Daltrey, R. With Hildred, S., *Thanks A Lot, Mr. Kibblewhite* (Henry Holt, New York, 2018)
Dolby, T., *The Speed Of Sound: Breaking The Barriers Between Music And Technology: A Memoir* (Flatiron Books, New York, 2016)
Downing, K.K., *Heavy Duty: Days And Nights In Judas Priest* (Constable, London, 2018)
Ellen, M., *Rock Stars Stole My Life!: A Big Bad Love Affair With Music* (Coronet, London, 2014)
Evans, J., *Rock & Pop On British TV* (Omnibus Press, London, 2017)
Flynn, R., (ed) *Classic Pop Presents 1984* 'Band Aid At 40' (Anthem Publishing, London, 2023)
Frith, S., Brennan, M., Cloonan, M. And Webster, E., *The History Of Live Music In Britain, Volume 3, 1985-2015* (Routledge, London, 2021)
Gaines, S., *Heroes And Villains: The True Story Of The Beach Boys* (Macmillan, London, 1986)
Geldof, B., *Is That It?* (Sidgwick And Jackson, London, 1986)
Graham, B. And Greenfield, R., *Bill Graham Presents: My Life Inside Rock And Out* (Da Capo, Cambridge, 2004)
Heylin, C., *Behind The Shades – 20th Anniversary Edition* (Faber And Faber, London, 2011)
Harvey, O., *Feed The World* (New Holland, London, 2013)
Hillmore, P., *Live Aid – The Concert* (Shuckburgh Reynolds, London, 1985)
Hynde, C., *Reckless: My Life As A Pretender* (Ebury Press, London, 2015)
Illsley. J., *My Life In Dire Straits: The Inside Story Of One Of The Biggest Bands In Rock History* (Diversion Books, New York, 2021)
Jobling, J., *U2: The Definitive Biography* (Thomas Dunne, New York, 2014)
John, E., *Me* (Henry Holt & Company, New York City, 2019)
Jones, D., *The Eighties: One Day, One Decade* (Windmill Books, London, 2013)
--- *David Bowie: A Life* (Windmill Books, London, 2018)
Jones, L.A., *Freddie Mercury: The Definitive Biography* (Hodder And

Stoughton, London, 2012)
Kelly, M., *Marillion, Misadventures & Marathons: The Life & Times Of Mad Jack* (Kingmaker, London, 2022)
Kemp, G., *I Know This Much* (Harpercollins, London, 2009)
Kemp, M., *True* (Orion Media, London, 2000)
Kershaw, A., *No Off Switch* (Serpent's Tail, London, 2011)
Love, M., *Good Vibrations: My Life As A Beach Boy* (Faber & Faber, London, 2017)
Nash, G., *Wild Tales* (Random House, New York, 2013)
Osbourne, O. And Ayres, A., *I Am Ozzy (*Grand Central Publishing, New York, 2010)
Paton, D., *Magic: The David Paton Story* (Sonicbond, Tewkesbury, 2023)
Rees, P., *The Ox* (Constable, London, 2020)
Rossi, F. *I Talk Too Much* (Little Brown, London, 2019)
Richards, K., *Life* (Little Brown, Boston, 2010)
Santana, C., *The Universal Tone: Bringing My Story To Light* (Little Brown, Boston, 2014)
Smith, S., *George* (Harpercollins, London, 2017)
Springfield, R., *Late, Late At Night: A Memoir* (Touchstone, New York, 2010)
Sting, *Broken Music: A Memoir* (Dial Press, New York, 2003)
Taraborrelli, J.R., *Madonna: An Intimate Biography* (Sidgwick & Jackson, London, 2001)
Townshend, P., *Who I Am* (Harpercollins, London, 2012)
Turner, T., *My Love Story* (Atria Books, New York City, 2019)
Ure, M., *If I Was* (Virgin Books, London, 2004)
Ware, M., *Electronically Yours: Vol. I: My Autobiography* (Constable, London, 2023)
Wilson, B., *I Am Brian Wilson: A Memoir* (Da Capo, Boston, 2016)
Wood, R., *Ronnie* (Macmillan, London, 2007)
Young, N., *Waging Heavy Peace: A Hippie Dream* (Penguin, New York, 2012)
--- *Special Deluxe: A Memoir Of Life And Cars* (Penguin, New York, 2014)
Zanes, W., *Tom Petty: The Biography* (Henry Holt, New York, 2015)
Zimmer, D., *Crosby, Stills And Nash: The Biography* (Da Capo, Boston, 3rd Edition, 2008)